DREAMING ANARCHY

ALAN MCMANUS

COPYRIGHT

First published in Scotland, 2015
Copyright © 2015 Alan McManus

ISBN-10: 1514362619
ISBN-13: 978-1514362617

Acknowledgements

¡Gracias a mis compañer@s en la lucha: Gora Okupak!
Grateful thanks to my family and friends and backpacking buddies of the Willy Wallace Hostel, Stirling, for support, belief and outrageous parties. To Dave for houseroom and hilarity. To Herman for lessons in transgender. To the secretaries, past and present, of the Department of Religious Studies, Stirling University, for their smiles, their help and their humanity. To the guys in the Computer Help Desk for assistance with the scanner. To my supervisor for helpful comments, and for permission to expand the word length! Thanks also to Ron Sanderson who has released the photo "Man's Back", which I use for my front cover, into the Public Domain: his work can be found at http://www.publicdomainpictures.net/browse-author.php?a=32182

"whether the anthropological study of the 'other' will necessarily one day embrace the researcher's own unconscious has yet to be seen, although Caplan [1] has suggested, in her discussion of 'engendering knowledge' that: ["]... the time has come for us all, male and female, to recognise that the sense of self which has sustained the practice of ethnography for so long is irrelevant and that as the French poet Rimbaud put it '*Je est un autre*' (1988:17)["]" (Edgar/1994/10)

[1] Caplan, P. (1988) "Engendering Knowledge: The Politics of Ethnography (Part 2)" in *Anthropology Today* 4, 6:14 –17.

CONTENTS

Introduction

Ch.1 Background: Contested Cartography

Ch.2 Anthropological Perspectives: Colonialism, Change and Resistance

Ch.3 Self-Consciousness and Self-Fashioning

Ch.4 Freud in Crisis: Theory, Methodology and Values

Ch.5 Preliminary Ethnographic Information

    i) *Euskal Herria* ii) *Libertari@s*
    iii) *Okupa* iv) *Community*

Excursus A: The Visit of the *Forales*

Excursus B: Dividing the Task: Housework and Genderplay

Ch.6 Conscious and Unconscious Character Description

    i) Erkametza ii) Chinebro

Ch.7 Monsters from the *Id*: Racism, Revenge and *Erotica*

Ch.8 Oneirocritical Methodology – a Shut Eye View

Ch.9 Conclusion

Introduction

I publish this book fourteen years after it was written as a Master's dissertation and, rereading it now, I realise how much the world has changed. In 2001 (anti)social media had hardly started and an even more clunky prototype was the cameraphone which had just been invented, was very expensive, and would take years to enter the ever-cheaper mobile phone market. The youth of the post-industrial countries appeared to be going through an all-time low in political activity and I distinctly remember that the only issue which appeared to rouse the President of the one Student Union in my 'oldest of the new' Scottish university (who went on to run the UK National Union of Students) was the rise in car parking charges. Postcolonialism was the new academic thing and no-one was talking about austerity. Students had started to graduate in debt but not to the extent that their undergraduate enslavement to meaningless call centre work had left them no time to study anything but the bare minimum to pass exams and that their graduate prospects were limited to supervisory positions in the same. LGB groups were just adding the 'T', no-one I knew applied the prefix 'cis' to any term other than 'alpine Gaul' – and for those few precious days after the destruction of the Twin Towers (before they started bombing the hell out of anyone with a beard and sandals) everyone loved America.

What I most treasure from my time with the back-to-nature community up in the Pyrenees was the silence. The absence of 'the voices' which daily babble to us in cities, relentlessly, from TV, Tablet, radio, mobile phone, iPod, LED, traffic light, checkout…and the absence of the internalised urge to buy, at any cost, in order to validate our identity as autonomous individuals in the faceless mass of globalised marketing. I also treasure the distant memory of privacy. We were not in danger of our every spontaneous expression being uploaded and photoshopped for the consumption of people we had never met and never would. My reasons for this study were suspected then and my reasons for publication may be suspected now. Such suspicion is understandable and has informed both the content of this book and the timing of its publication. The world has changed, in many ways for the worse, and I have changed with it but another world is still possible and for a time I was privileged to be part of that change for the better. Perhaps that change does not need to have such an oppositional relationship to the state that it constantly endangers its own existence. Perhaps too technology, without sacrifice of serenity, may play a part in realising bucolic dreams.

In two telling passages in her article on "Rereading *Zen and the Art of Motorcycle Maintenance*", Louise Harmon (2013/19n.32,29) cites the kind of social distraction and focus solely on grades that interfere with educational attention today:

"I sat in an Evidence class and watched two law students in front of me pretend to take notes on their computers. One was on Facebook, looking over a gallery of remarkably raunchy pictures from a recent bacchanalia. The other was buying a dress for a formal affair."

"we deliver a deeply felt, extemporaneous soliloquy on the meaning of life, and a student (in the front row) raises his hand and wants to know, "Will that be on the exam?" "

In this situation today of the ability to learn being so challenged, my innovative methodology of mnemonic excellence, using dreams as sticky webs of meaning, may be of timely help.

My hope is that people will be inspired by these reflections on a community where everyone worked, everyone was provided for and money hardly existed, where learning and teaching were as natural as the organic food and where global empathy inspired action that was truly local, and political ideology relationships that were truly personal. We, as I came to dream us, did not wait for a revolution in order to turn to each other, to turn back to the land, to turn our hands to tasks communal and individual with skills old and newly-learned. In doing so, our anger at the destruction of our communities and our planet, by the impersonal evil of disaster capitalism, informed our way of life but it was not our overriding motivation. Instead we were inspired by a trinity of values that have defined anarchy more truly than any nihilistic destruction: mutual aid, spontaneity and love. These values are freely available to all and all are welcome to build communities based on them. We can remember how to build sustainable communities; if we can't remember, we can invent; and if we don't know how, we can dream ourselves into action.

Chapter 1 Background: Contested Cartography

In the autumn of 2001 I spent four months in the Iberian Peninsula doing fieldwork in an *okupa* community of *libertari@s* [2] near Iruñea/ Pamplona, and writing up and reading anarchist theory and Iberian anthropology in Granada, Andalusia. My initial project was to attempt an ethnography, notwithstanding the very short period. My near-native grasp of Castilian Spanish and my familiarity with the philosophy and indeed some of the members of the community from previous visits encouraged this optimism. Concerns voiced by the community about confidentiality and academia called for a sensitive methodology. This was in tune with my own desire to write ethnopoetry (I have two anarchist poems on the community published in the Peninsula) inspired by the work of Hubert Fichte (1987) *Etnopoesía: Antropologia Poética das Religiões Afro-Americanas*, on *Macumba* in Brazil. I combined this with an (Italian) renaissance pedagogy of *poesía commentata*, which I had studied in the Spanish mystical poetry of san Juan de la Cruz.

I have lived in several, diverse, communities, several facts endeared me immediately to this particular one, which I shall call Erkametza [3]: I had known one of its members (whom I've named "Ricardo") over a period of two years, when we studied together at the University of Granada and when I visited him in two other *okupa* communities, also in the Pyrenees; I was used to community life, 'roughing it' and working on organic farms; I was in the process of bitter conflict with the Dept. of Religious Studies of my university over fair funding, grading and staff professionalism and I made great scones!

My previous sojourn in the Peninsula had culminated in 18 months utilising Freudian methodology to read poetry as dream. I felt that *The Interpretation of Dreams* might be useful in dissolving the emic/ etic division and foregrounding the process of identification/ rejection undergone by the ethnographer in the community as well as highlighting the fractured and/ or relational self. The process of using this alternative methodology in the field (quite literally!) brought up a number of questions, considering the appropriateness of my methodology, which I decided to explore as *prolegomena*:

i) From a postcolonial perspective what "Mediterranean" stereotypes may influence a northern European ethnographer studying anywhere in Spanish Territory?

ii) What do theories on the 'self' contribute to a self-aware methodology?

iii) Is anything of value in Sigmund Freud's Interpretation of Dreams?

iv) How adequate is a bi-polar division of gender and of work/non-work?

v) How should dreams with difficult and offensive matter be interpreted and reported?

My purpose is neither to attempt a complete ethnography (whatever that may be apart from cultural arrogance!) nor to exhaustively answer all these questions. Instead I will illustrate the perspective of an oneirocritical methodology on the ethnographer, the community studied and the relationship between them; and discuss the effect of this on an ethnography.

NOTES

[2] The "@" is one of the strategies of Spanish anarco-punk feminist orthography. All Spanish nouns and adjectives show a binary division of gender: this "@" neutralises gender and visually privileges the feminine "a" as well as referring to the anarchist capital "A" in a circle. Hooper (1995/284) speaks of the "use of a 'k' … [as] one of the orthographic innovations employed by the founder of Basque nationalism, Sabino Arana, to differentiate Basque from Spanish, and for recent generations it has come to symbolize Basque rejectionism.". My ethnopoem, the original of "A Perfect Anarchist" uses this orthography.

[3] I also spent ten days in a sister community, Chinebro. See discussion in the Methodology section, just before Dream 14 (xiv).

Chapter 2 Anthropological Perspectives: Colonialism, Change and Resistance.

Anthropology has come a long way since Mead, Malinowsky and Radcliffe-Brown and is – at least – aware of its cultural imperialism. Edward Said has shown that "Orientalism is … a sign of European-Atlantic power over the Orient" (Said 1995/6) and cites the use of a description of a village in Egypt to describe one in Syria (*op cit*/23). Josep Llobrera has a similar critique of the sign "Mediterranean"[4] and speaks of "the Myth of Carmen" whose 'Mediterranean' characteristics are clearly not to be found in either Catalonia or the Piedmont. While the danger of imperialist generalisation is clear, comparison may be helpful if each example is interrogated as to its dissimilarity as well as to its similitude.

I was attracted to Geertz' (2000) "thick description" and ethnography as "deep hanging out" and Clifford's (1997) work on transient populations. I was also influenced by the experiences of a growing number of – mainly female – ethnographers such as Donner (1982) and Cesara (1982) who, in foregrounding the integration process do not see this process simply as a step towards the real goal (objective data) nor a hindrance. Instead, as the ethnographer develops more emotional bonds with the community the research becomes at once more subjective, more nuanced and complex. Geertz defines the "study of other peoples' cultures" as "discovering who they think they are, what they think they are doing, and to what end they think they are doing it". (Geertz/*op cit*/16) Llobrera declares that Geertz' *"renuncia a la tarea científica de la antropología, al legado de generaciones de antropólogos que consagraron su existencia al progreso de la disciplina, sitúa a Geertz fuera de las murallas antropológicas stictu sensu."*[5]

No doubt there is substance to Llobrera's complaint that Geertz' conflation of (social) anthropology and ethnography is justified (*op cit*, p. 39) and that in 'thick description' *"el bosque de la descripción no deja ver los arboles de la precisión fatica,"*[6] but his excommunication of Geertz is overdone. I welcome Llobrera's postcolonial (?) critique of 'the ethnography of the Mediterranean' but the same de-bunking process can be applied to much of the *"dos siglos de antropología como ciencia"*[7] which he observes Geertz unfairly throwing out. Robert Young in *Colonial Desire: Hybridity in Theory, Culture, and Race* (1995) has convincingly shown that anthropology needs a great deal of its 'scientific legacy' thrown out as bad ideas backed by an army. Furthermore to this argument, if Geertz and Llobrera are championing a right brain/ left brain methodology respectively then science nowadays (as in pre-Enlightenment days) can sit happily in either hemisphere and especially in their connection.

Can what Kitcher (1992) warned of in interdisciplinary sciences be a helpful corrective here? That such sciences, basing their epistemology on other ('hard') sciences must constantly check and keep up to date with developments in those supporting bases otherwise the whole edifice falls?[8] Llobrera's simplistic nomenclature of *"la antropología subjetiva, interpretiva o dialógica, o como se quiera llamarla"*[9] ignores everything since Einstein about the effect of the observer on the system observed. If Geertz can, tongue in cheek, state: "Everyone knew that … the Tepotzlanos [were] either unshakeably unified or hopelessly divided (there were two anthropologists who studied them, one the student of the other)" (Geertz/2000/12,13) then my questions would be: Did they hate each other? Did one cut off the other's funding and the latter take ethnographic revenge? What moods were they in most of the time? Did they like the Tepotzlanos? How were they dressing, eating, speaking, working and who were they attracted to and what differences did all that make to the community?

Ethnography Step by Step (Fetterman, 1998) recommends choosing between a mentalist and a physicalist theory of anthropology – as a first step. Also called cognitive/idealist or materialist, the author considers this division as a given in social science. From Plato to Pirsig these contending options and their related aesthetics, Classical and Romantic (or Apollonian and Dionysian, as named by Nietzsche [see Paglia/1990]) have waged war: the former concerned with underlying form and the latter with outward appearance. However in my general reading of recent anthropological accounts, I feel that both approaches are important for the apprehension of the Gestalt experienced in the Field.

Kurt Lewin, commenting on the "variety of facts which social psychology has to treat" and listing examples ["values", "ideologies", "cultural", "psychological", "physiological", "physical"] states that "it is utterly fruitless and merely a negative scientific treatment to put these facts into classificatory pigeonholes... we need positive means of bringing these various types of facts together in such a way that one can treat them on one level without sacrificing the recognition of their specific characteristics." (Lewin/1967/133) He recommends a "field-theoretical approach ...[as] a practical vehicle of research" (*op cit*/134) Using this approach to discuss "the problem of adolescence" (*op cit*/149), Lewin feels that " a way must be found to treat bodily changes, shift of ideology, and group-belongingness within one realm of scientific language, in a single realm of discourse." His method utilises "constructs which characterise objects and events in terms of interdependence rather than phenotypical similarity or dissimilarity." (*ibid*) He goes onto an example of a concrete research methodological problem in the field of adolescence ["whether or not one is permitted to combine concepts of values with those of bodily weight"] which "vanishes when confronted with the simple truth that both facts influence the same situation." (*ibid*).

Iain Ross Edgar's work on dream groups (1994) was interesting as at first I wondered if we were doing something similar. However, as the following quote shows, he is very definitely using a mentalist approach:

"The base of my study is a "psychoethnography" as Obeyeskere (1990:xx) defines the study of the transformation of symbolic forms from and into culture. The base of the ethnography is a textual construction of the dream reports and the process of developing meaning in emic terms by the group members. Such a 'thick description' shows the creation of the 'webs of significance' that Geertz (1973:5)[10] defines as 'culture'. 'Psychoethnography' cannot see the description of a material universe or a set of economic and political realities as its main task. Rather I describe the processual construction of meaning in a group setting." (Edgar/1994/12)

From my (hopefully) more holistic approach both "economic and political realities" as well as "symbolic forms" come clearly into focus. I have mentioned other ethnographers but perhaps I was most inspired in my presentation of ethnographic material by Margery Wolf, who, in, *A thrice–told tale: feminism, postmodernism, and*

7

ethnographic responsibility (1992) used field diary, short story and standard anthropologyspeak to tell her tale, bringing out different aspects of an dramatic incident in a village in Taiwan.

NOTES

[4] "*La etnografía del Mediterráneo constituyó su propio objeto al crear comunidades sin historia ni milieu.*" "The ethnography of the Mediterranean constituted its own object by creating communities with neither history nor *milieu*." (Llobrera/1990/80)

[5] "renunciation of the scientific task of anthropology, of the legacy of generations to the progress of the discipline, situates Geertz outside the walls of anthropology in the strict sense." (Llobrera/1990/43)

[6] "the forest of description doesn't allow the trees of factual precision to be seen," (Llobera/1990/40)

[7] "two centuries of anthropology as science" (Llobrera/1990/34)

[8] Paraphrase of Kitcher's entire thesis, see her critique of Freud which I discuss below.

[9] "subjective, interpretive or dialogic ethnography, or however one would wish to name it" Llobrera/1990/34.

[10] Geertz, C. (1973) "Thick description: Towards an Interpretative Theory of Culture" in *The Interpretation of Cultures*. New York. Basic Books.

Chapter 3 Self–Consciousness and Self–Fashioning.

In my own research I have attempted to realise the self-consciousness that Cohen urges by highlighting my own and other's self-fashioning. In a series of quotes Edgar establishes the accepted party line in Cultural Studies [12] on the 'self':

"The mainly anthropological perspectives that I use begin, as I have discussed, with Tedlock's communicative theory of dreams.[13] This situates my focus on dream narrating as a cultural process, firmly in the social, and I would argue as constituting the embodiment paradigm derived from Merleau-Ponty and Bourdieu, and explicated in Csordas (1990).[14] This presents the self as an integrated mind/ body in reality inseparable from the social creation by which the subject is both generating and being generated (Csordas 1990:10). Moreover Csordas, following Merleau-Ponty (1962:238–9), [15] asserts that not only are the reflective self and its cognitive processes culturally constructed, but experience prior to a reflective and abstract understanding is also culturally formed. He develops Merleau-Ponty's concept of the "preobjective or prereflexive" to express this idea (1990;10). Csordas also suggests that Bourdieu's concept of habitus can be subsumed within the concept of the 'preobjective'. For Bourdieu the body is similarly not an object within a world of objects, but rather a 'socially informed body' (1977:124)[16] generating meaningful interaction through its 'perduring dispositions' (1977:72)." (Edgar/1994/11)

Just how much I had accepted the 'self' as socially constructed was brought home to me on reading *Self Consciousness: An Alternative Anthropology of Identity* (1994) by Anthony Cohen. It caused me to review my experience and especially as I had lived with such a small group I could see the strength of his argument that we should:

"regard social groups as a collection of complex selves… they are more complicated and require more subtle and sensitive description than if we treat them as a combination of roles. Indeed, the aggregation of these complex entities into groups may itself be seen as more problematic than would otherwise be the case. Collective

9

behaviour is then revealed as something of a triumph, rather than as being merely mechanical." (Cohen/1994/7). "How can you discriminate between the other person's consciousness and your construction of his or her consciousness?...[he admits] 'I cannot'... this admission... calls into question the methodological pretensions of modern anthropology. It amounts to the admission that the inevitable starting point for my interpretation of another's selfhood is my own self." (*op cit*/3).

In the epilogue to "Renaissance Self–Fashioning", Stephen Greenblatt seems to have the empirical evidence against Cohen and for Edgar:

"Whenever I focused sharply upon a moment of apparently autonomous self–fashioning, I found not an epiphany of identity freely chosen but a cultural artefact. If there remained traces of free choice, the choice was among possibilities whose range was strictly delineated by the social and ideological system in force. The book I have written reflects these perceptions, but I trust that it also reflects, though in a manner more tentative, more ironic than I had originally intended, my initial impulse. For all the sixteenth-century Englishmen I have written about here do in fact cling to the human subject and to self–fashioning, even in suggesting the absorption or corruption or loss of the self...As for myself...I want to bear witness at the close to my overwhelming need to sustain the illusion that I am the principal maker of my own identity." (Greenblatt/1984/256–257).

Fascinating though the above-quoted book is, I wonder (in a post-colonial aside) whether part of its appeal and the reason for the reverential tone in which it is usually spoken of in Cultural Studies (and especially in English Departments) is an ideological re-establishment of a reassuringly English canon (with London as central metropolis) hallowed by time and cultural imperialism. Is it in fact a move away from Lyotard and back to Leavis? [see Barry/1995/28–29] Whatever the truth of my caricature, Greenblatt's conclusion may be even more nuanced by Cohen's review of "cultural theories of the self" which shows the "illusion" to be on the part of the social scientist:

"in which individuals are depicted as (i) constrained by the structural imperatives of their political roles (Goffman; Bailey); (ii) supported (or inhibited) by their structurally superior statuses (or lack of them) (Bloch); (iii) the agents of their own success, either because of their persuasiveness (Paine), their oratorical prowess (Atkinson) or their sensitivity to the use of appropriate cultural idioms (Parkin). If these positions were plotted on a scale of personal discretion, (i) and (ii) would be negative; (iii) would be positive. There seems to have frequently been a confusion here between two distinct matters: the cultural recognition of selfhood – that is, the existence within a culture of a concept which may be regarded as an approximation to 'self' – and the discretion allowed to an individual to be individualistic or even merely to be self conscious." (Cohen/1994/51)

NOTES

[12] My Master's course was Religious Studies officially but had a lot in common with the materialistic assumptions of Cultural Studies.

[13] Tedlock, B. (1987a) "Dreaming and Dream Research" in B.Tedlock (Ed.) *Dreaming: Anthropological and Psychological Interpretations*. Cambridge. Cambridge University Press.

[14] Csordas, T (1990) Embodiment as a Paradigm for Anthropology. *Ethos*, 8:5–47.

[15] Merleau-Ponty, M, (1962) *The Primacy of Perception*. Evanston, IL: Northwest University Press.

[16] Bourdieu, P. (1977) *Outline of a Theory of Practice*. Cambridge: Cambridge University Press.

Chapter 4 Freud in Crisis: Theory, Methodology and Values.

The self-conscious methodology that I adopted was to record and analyse my own dreams while in the community, using *The Interpretation of Dreams* as a toolbox. I hoped to observe not only the transition from English (and Scots) to Spanish (and Basque) but also the *Gestalt* of resistance and attraction to my self-definition as a member of the community. Using Freud's theory of everyday events stimulating appearances in dreams, my dream analysis will necessarily include substantial ethnographic material of a more traditional kind. Thus my ethnography will be an example of the double-discourse of Symbolic/ Semiotic coined by Julia Kristeva and while not pretending to objectivity, will highlight the selection of data and hypotheses which "objective" studies do not. My data will be my dreams, a fitting form with which to study a utopia.

Patricia Kitcher's subtitle of *Freud's Dream: A Complete Interdisciplinary Science of Mind* indicates her belief that Freud too was interested in 'a single realm of discourse' [Lewin, cited above] in fact in "the synthesis of the mental sciences at the end of the last century" (Kitcher/1992/219). However she feels that "the unsavoury reputation of psychoanalysis is due largely to Freud's misunderstanding of the interdisciplinary structure of his theory." Even so, she feels that "perhaps psychoanalysis still has substantive insights to offer in the fields of personality and motivation, and even in anthropology and sociology." Kitcher is not certainly not alone in voicing a wariness in using Freud, Richard Webster's tome *Why Freud was Wrong* (1995) basically describes Freud as a secularised 'religious' megalomaniac but even Webster concludes that:

"the intellectual estate of psychoanalysis is a large and complex one which contains, amid much theoretical poverty and intellectual bric-a-brac, a small quantity of the gold of true psychological insight." (Webster /1995/509)

I have neither the psychological knowledge nor the inclination to refute this damning by faint praise except to state that in terms of dream detective work Freud talks a good line. Camille Paglia shares this appreciation, in her usual hyperbolic style:

"Spenser, Shakespeare and Freud are the three greatest sexual psychologists in literature, continuing a tradition begun by Euripides and Ovid. Freud has no rivals among his successors [she famously advised followers of Lacan to "THINK!"] because they think he wrote science, when in fact he wrote art."(Paglia/1990/228)

A cursory glance at the established canon of Critical Theory will reveal that it is *de rigueur* to cite Jacques Lacan as if it were that only this fashionable lens could bring the fuzzy performance of Freud's opera into focus. While I do not share Camille Paglia's outright rejection of Lacan's work, I do feel that it is an interesting misreading of Freud which lacks the high resolution and disciplined gaze of his analysis.[16] One of the principles of scientific research is verifiability: in this study I limit my choice of lens to that of Freud in *The Interpretation of Dreams*; publish my dreams and selected analyses and forswear other readings so as to foreground the Freudian reading which can thus be verified or challenged. I am neither a psychologist nor an unquestioning adherent of Freud. Cognisant of the many flaws and ethical problems with his theory (not least his hetero/sexism) I nonetheless feel that his work on latent and manifest content of dreams has yet to be surpassed. Freud summarises his theory of dreamwork (mental processes of the person while dreaming: not while undergoing analysis, *pace* Edgar!) as:

"investigating the relations between the manifest content of dreams and the latent dream–thoughts, and of tracing out the processes by which the latter have been changed into the former. The dream thoughts and the dream content are presented to us like two versions of the same subject-matter in two different languages... The dream-thoughts are immediately comprehensible, as soon as we have learned them. The dream-content, on the other hand, is expressed as it were in a pictographic script, the characters of which have to be transposed individually into the language of the dream-thoughts." (Freud/ 1988/381)

This pictorial script gives rise to Freud's use of symbols and also the dramatisation which is the "grammar" of the manifest content. By "condensation" Freud means "the amount of compression that has taken place" (*op cit*/282) in the dream narrative (e.g.

compression of time, space and people/objects), while "over-determination" signifies that "each of the elements of the dream's content turns out to have been 'over-determined' – to have been represented in the dream-thoughts many times over." (*op cit*/ 389)

An example of condensation is that of all the different women that Freud was thinking about, making "Irma" (in his dream of her [*op cit*/182]) an over-determined figure as an attribute from each women ("position by the window"; "diphtheritic membrane"; "name"; "recalcitrance over opening her mouth" etc.) is displaced onto this figure – the only one to appear in the manifest content. In displacement an attribute may also be reversed for further disguise ('up' equals 'down' etc. and this serves to further over-determine the figure or action).[17] The last of "the factors concerned in the construction of dreams...[is]...secondary revision" (*op cit*/629)[18] which is when:

"the psychical agency which otherwise operates only as a censorship plays a [ ] part in the construction of dreams.[19] [The dreamer's censor] fills up the gaps in the dream-structure...[so that] the dream loses its appearance of absurdity and disconnectedness and approximates to the model of an intelligible experience." (Freud/*op cit*/630)

My Freudian reading therefore consists in accepting his basic premise that dreams are wish-fulfilments **[20]** although I grant with Osborne (1993/111,2) that the introduction of the concept of *Thanatos* (as opposed to *Eros*) complicates this, unless desire is seen as often also sadistic or masochistic (see most of Paglia's opus). I then use his forensic interrogation of the dream in reference to the events of the previous day and the concerns of the dreamer (see Freud/1888/247) in order to reverse the dream-work processes of: condensation; displacement; over-determination; and secondary revision so as to observe the latent content of dream-thoughts. Osborne paraphrases one of Eysenck's criticisms of Freud as "Freud was against quantification (statistics) which produces vagueness."[21]

The Interpretation of Dreams is indeed not a work of statistics but in it Freud, with logical progression, expounds his theories, elucidating them with selected illustrations. His dream analyses can

14

be challenged but not all of these challenges run counter to his theories: the dream of Irma noted above can be read as extremely sexual with the symbolism of the "dirty injection" and a gang of men around a woman coercing her to open her mouth! In the same way my published self-analyses will leave levels of analysis unread (or unwritten) either from personal reserve, resistance, omission as inappropriate to the study, concerns of confidentiality or simple oversight and thus are open to other readings, verifying (or not) my conclusions.

Edgar seems to confuse analysis with 'dreamwork', a very specific Freudian word:

"Dreamwork then became for Freudian analysis the bringing to light, through free association, of the repressed aspects of the self." (Edgar/1994/45)

The definition of 'dreamwork' is important, otherwise in the following quotation one may get the impression that 'secondary process thinking' (secondary revision) only occurs in the waking state, whereas Freud has it as one of the four factors of dream construction [see above]. Edgar appears to believe that latent content equals primary process thinking and manifest, secondary; which is quite wrong:

"Freud also elaborated the important distinction between primary process and secondary process thinking. Primary process thought is for Kracke, "a highly condensed, visual, or sensory, metaphorical form of thinking". Secondary process thinking is defined as conscious, "centered on language and is linguistically communicable" (1987:38). Dreaming is for Freud, par excellence, primary process thought which he regarded as a more primitive form of thinking which also formed the core of myths and fairytales. Such an important distinction has however been challenged and Kracke reviews this debate, concluding that; ["]Primary process thought is a qualitatively different kind of thought from secondary process and is just as much subject to maturation and refinement as the latter["] (1987:37–40)" (Edgar/1994/45)

Kracke's above definitions are useful if their specific Freudian use is borne in mind but his last quotation makes no sense as the process of "maturation and refinement" is precisely what the secondary process does to the primary! This next quote may explain:

"Freud's pioneering work on the psyche and the role and function of the unconscious is extremely well known and many of his insights have passed, not always exactly, into the popular culture of understanding dreams." (Edgar/1994/45, emphasis mine.)

However I do agree with Edgar's comments on *bricolage* and this is in fact the main use I make of the dreams to observe the ethnographic data they accrue:

"as myth for Levi–Strauss is a form of *bricolage* (1966:17) so the dream for Kracke is a form of bricolage which gathers, ["]from among the day residues ready to hand, and uses them to express metaphorically an emotional conflict, and to work out (or work toward) some resolution of it["] (1987:38)" (Edgar/1994/7)**[22]**

NOTES

[16] "Not only does Lacan engage in a baroque linguistic rhetoric that makes *Nostradamus* seem clear, he also went in for algebraic formulae that add up to the clarity of Hades." (Osbourne/1993/160) "So we have this strange phenomenon of the radical Lacan rewriting Freud through language and yet ending up with a position in which anatomy is destiny, only now (langanatomy) the word is imprisonment." (*Op cit*/164)
[17] See this reversal with allusions to Sappho/ wet-nurse/ Lesbians/ homosexual desire (Freud/1888/394)
[18] Osborne (1993) has "secondary elaboration".
[19] Freud/1888/629. The word omitted is *"habitual"* which Freud sees as the frequency (not the condition) of this factor.
[20] " 'What' asks the proverb, 'do geese dream of?' And it replies: 'Of maize.' The whole theory that dreams are wish-fulfilments is contained in these two phrases." (Freud/1888/212).

[21] From Eysenck's *The Rise and Fall of the Freudian Empire*, cited in Osborne (1993/143)

[22] Levi-Strauss, C. (1966) *The Savage Mind*. Chicago, IL: University of Chicago Press. Kracke, W. (1987) "Myths in Dreams, Thought in Images: An Amazonian Contribution to the Psychoanalytic Theory of Process." In B.Tedlock (Ed.) *Dreaming: Anthropological and Psychological Interpretations*. Cambridge: Cambridge University Press.

Chapter 5 Preliminary Ethnographic Information

(i) *Euzkal Herria*

Euzkal Herria, like the Scottish *Ghaidhealtach*, defines a geographical area of land according to the language spoken there. Even though Castilian Spanish may be the dominant language numerically and in terms of political discourse, (especially after the *Franquista* policy of saturation with Andalusian factory workers) *Euzkal Herria* is where *Euzkadi* is spoken. The geographical area is coterminal with the 'Spanish' and 'French' Basque Country but also includes that historically singular 'Foral' community, Navarre.

The heraldic shield of Navarre is bordered and crossed by chains symbolising the *Fueros*, the ancient laws of the province which have caused the Spanish statute books to be filled with explicit inclusion or exclusion of Navarre. Manipulation of this legislative double discourse of Foral Law and Spanish Law have enabled the provincial government to resist directives from Madrid and continue with the building of a reservoir which has caused bitter polemic since the 1950's.[23] Typical of the centralist campaign of General Franco, an oppression of alterity in Spanish Territory which began with the '*reconquista*' of the '*Reyes Católicos*', thousands of people in little towns and villages in the Pyrenees were forced from their homes with the compulsory purchase orders (grossly undervaluing property) and physical violence which for me was reminiscent of the Scottish Highland Clearances. From the 1980's, a decade of greater social upheaval in Spanish Territory than the 1960's and '70's, groups of young people began to re-occupy these (mostly bulldozed) villages, encountering legal opposition and popular support as they did so.

Euzkal Herria's most famous (indeed infamous) popular opposition to Spanish centralism is ETA, and many Basques are quick to publicly distance themselves from this Maoist revolutionary group by deploring its violent means while still supporting its political aims. The political tension created by this low level and unofficial civil war of terrorism, torture, intimidation and fear is such that the Guardia Civil is perceived as especially heavy handed in *Euzkal Herria* where their brutality is surpassed only by the *Forales*. As Spain has, like Britain, chosen to pander to the irresponsibility of a US politics of paranoia following the events of 'September 11th' 2001, any non-centralist discourse is immediately suspect. Although always centralist, the earliest *Franquista* politics of fascism did not support either the monarchy or the Church. Franco subsequently changed policy so completely that he is said to have died saying that "*España no estará sin mi, yo continuo en la persona del Rey*"[24] ETA was famously born in a seminary [25] – perhaps the only place where such a subversive group could escape civil surveillance – and the clergy in *Euzkal Herria*, despite their repeated condemnation of violence, have strong Basque nationalist leanings.[26]

However, the myth of '*las dos Españas*': one fascist, monarchical and catholic; the other anarchist/ communist and atheist, is also operative in *Euzkal Herria*. Although the Church in *Euzkal Herria* supported the Republic,[27] Navarre supported Franco and alone in *Euzkal Herria* keeps its oppressive Foral Law which the clergy had fought for during the *Carlista* wars of the late 19th C.[28]

(ii) *Libertari@s*

A libertarian praxis was one of the major discourses of the left wing of the Spanish Civil War – the other being state communism. Young people today who identify themselves as '*progres*' (progressives) are well versed in this history and often use Rastafarian dreadlocks, clothing made of natural fibres and communal smoking of marijuana or hashish to visibly recognise each other and be distinct from the more formal, conservative look of right-wing youth. Political apathy is not unknown in young people but (unlike Britain) it is unusual.[29] The relative formality of clothes in Spanish Territory as opposed to Britain (at least till recently, in both countries) may also cause confusion in the significance of dress codes. A more reliable indicator is music, Reggae in general and especially Manu Chau whose CDs of feelgood soft rock multilingual anthems are of significant iconographic value amongst the *progre* youth of the whole of the Iberian Peninsula and at least France and Italy.

During my two-year sojourn in Granada, I benefited from the knowledge and experience of a young man closely involved in the *Colectivo Nacional de Trabajadores*, one of the oldest and most influential of the *anarco-sindicalista* groups and was struck by the constant reference and relation of what CNT were doing today, to the anarchist praxis of the Civil War. While CNT seem to use the terms '*anarquista*' and '*comunista libertari@*' interchangeably, one young man in the community studied told me quite firmly that he was the latter but not the former. He was politically informed enough not to confuse 'anarchy' with 'chaos' (as do most uniformed anglophones) but may have felt that the former designation recalled the painful and politically suicidal split between anarchist and communist in the Civil War, which the latter term elides. Another member of the community, with similar political self-definition, described CNT as "old anarchist hard-liners" and indeed I have observed intense political rivalry between them and other left wing groups.

Although the 'Two Spains' myth tends to censure talk of 'organised' religion in libertarian company, there are a number of Catholics who are concerned with "Justice and Peace" issues – some of which overlap with a libertarian agenda – in broad outline and usually safely overseas.[30] Even the staunchly atheist in the community often found their political and familial allegiance in conflict over the pressure to be godparents, sponsors, or best man/ maid of honour/ bridesmaid or a reader at the Catholic liturgical rites of passage which are so publicly part of Peninsular life. Other *libertari@s* were agnostic and/or open to an eclectic mixture of Buddhist, Hermetic, Celtic and New Age spiritualities familiar to me from student bookshelves (including my own) in the UK. The libertarian lifestyle, although based on a professed philosophy of historical materialism has many characteristics of a spirituality. I would sometimes observe to libertarian friends that they were acting like Catholic martyrs in their *kenosis* of their vital energy for the cause. This usually caused not only amusement but also a juxtaposition of discourses which encouraged further reflection.

(iii) *Okupa*

To be an *okupa* is to occupy, in modern English 'to squat'.[31] A related discourse is *insumisión*, refusing to do military service – even the (longer) alternative of community work and one factor in *okupación* may be the need for the *insumis@* to live inconspicuously to avoid being drafted by force. Both *okupación* and *insumsión* are illegal, often incur intrusive, if not brutal, police/ military action and give instant street-cred. To be an *insumis@* you need to be a citizen and to be eligible to be called up and then to refuse: to be an *okupa* you need only occupy space which legally is not yours. The military has now been completely professionalised in all Spanish Territory but *okupación* goes on. Simply staying with the community made me technically an *okupa* and I narrowly avoided arrest when the *Forales* came to harass us one day. Interestingly, after they recognised me as an *okupa* (and I refused, to show them my passport), the community trusted me much more and I identified more with them.

A group of six woke up one winter morning in Aragón to find eighty "Rambos" who physically maltreated them then systematically smashed all their rebuilt houses, pottery shed, bakery and carpentry workshops before going on to slaughter poultry, trash the plants in the fields and scatter the animals.[32] The group then spent six weeks in an internment camp in the snow along with several other *okupa*s, among them women and babies. Most *okupa*s I met reported similar police/military harassment. As well as a criminal record, *okupación* also provides an experience of community in rent-free accommodation away from parental pressure.[33] If being an *okupa* has more street-cred than just being a *progre* it is because you are putting yourself in the line of fire (sometimes literally) of several oppositional discourses. In the community where I lived, we were not only illegal under Spanish Law but also under the *Fueros*. In addition to this, we were occupying land in a region which (although designated by Madrid as a Special Natural Reserve because of its indigenous, threatened fauna) was earmarked for deforestation and bulldozing because of plans to continue with the construction of a nearby dam. The Navarran Provincial Government were hand-in-glove with the company building the dam which had a political power and jurisdiction reminiscent of the East India Company.

Further to this unholy trinity of oppositional discourses, ETA had recently been targeting the *Forales*, justifying their killing with the slogan (in *Euskera*) "on traffic duty today: on torture duty tomorrow" and they in turn (urged by Madrid) were using anti-terrorist laws to harass *okupa*s. Basque nationalism and anarchism have historically not always seen eye to eye (as I have noted above) and while among individual *okupa*s there was debate over the relative merits of Basque independence and international socialism, there were no formal links between the two groups. Would terrorists would live in such high profile illegal communities when surely a better cover would be a more bland lifestyle?

(iv) Community

I had been overwhelmed on my previous visit with the amount of anarchist ideology in the posters on the walls of the Gaztetxe, the *okupa* social centre and meeting place in Iruñea. Ricardo had informed me on arrival that a collective decision had been taken by all the *okupa*s in the area of Iruñea not to allow any academic studies of them. The concerns were not simply that this information could be used by the police/ military/ dam company, but that they would have no control over their possible misrepresentation. Also, as anarchists, they viewed academia as a completely fascist discourse and given my rough-housing in the Department I wasn't inclined to disagree. I had anticipated this and had tailored my methodology not only to their concerns but to an area of expertise which I had developed in Granada (before I was thrown out by *Opus Dei* for doing a Freudian reading of the saintliest of Spanish saints) and which Ricardo was familiar with. He vouched for me and it was understood that not only would the focus of my research be on the ethnographer and not the community but that I would only disclose such information as was already known to the authorities.[34]

After the incident with the *Forales*, the questions about my work stopped but individuals would tell me their dreams for help in interpretation. All went well until I broached the topic of hierarchy at an *asamblea* (I had just broken up with my girlfriend in Barcelona and was not feeling too convivial) and the reaction of some of those who took most responsibility in the community made me decide on a study trip to Granada. In my absence the whole community underwent a course in consensus decision-making (influenced by a model from Findhorn, the New Age community near Inverness) during which the topic, among many others, was more tactfully raised and worked through.

In fact what I found remarkable about this community was exactly the anarchy, the liberty to do what one pleased and the love which grew out of the mutual aid and respect we practised daily. I only heard how loud the clamour of capitalism is when it was stilled. My senses, unnumbed by 'commodities' began to open up, my eyesight got better, intuition sharper and I learned that, in the absence of 'professionals' I could develop a variety of practical skills which – though far from perfect – worked. The community, unlike the university, was teaching me to learn and share skills.

NOTES

[23] See Dreams and ANALYSIS esp. Dream 2c note (vii)

[24] See Hooper (1995/31) on the accession of King Juan Carlos: "Kneeling down, with one hand resting on the New Testament, he swore loyalty to Franco and fidelity to the principles of the Movimiento Nacional."

[25] *ETA Nació en un Seminario*, "ETA was born in a Seminary", is a popular account of their origins.

[26] See Hooper (1995/16,17) on Spanish economic migrants to Bilbao and *Opus Dei*.

[27] See *ibid*. "In contrast to what happened in the rest of Spain [*sic*], the Basque clergy sided with the Republic during the civil war and paid the price for their choice after Franco's victory when sixteen of their number were executed" (*op cit*/137).

[28] See *op cit*/394, 395; 397 for the unique position of Navarre.

[29] To a non-hispanophone this may not be immediately apparent, such tourists (known pejoratively as '*guiris*') are not taken very seriously and are unlikely to hear confessions of political allegiance.

[30] A fellow worker with people with learning difficulties in Catalonia (where I spent a summer) told me that "the Church may be interested in justice but it's not interested in liberty". She was speaking about that region but the observation may be applied to Spanish Territory as a whole.

[31] *Okupación* has reached such numbers that a government minister described it as 'a plague on our youth'. (*El Pais*, December '02. I do not have the exact reference.)

[32] Sasé, February 2000, the case is famous in the Iberian Peninsula. Pancho and Ricardo were living there. I had visited this community one month before and written my first ethnopoem for them which was published in a peripatetic trans-Pyrenean exhibition that year. See Chinebro poem, below.

[33] Hooper (1995/285) only mentions *okupas* in terms of "the property boom of the late eighties" and the subsequent "plight of would-be couples".

[34] The authorities knew so much about the community that I probably could have come up with a standard ethnography after a couple of hours at the police station so the latter injunction was not hard to keep!

Excursus A: The Visit of the *Forales*

I include this part of the dream ANALYSIS of Dream 23 here as I have already referred to it and will again and it was crucial to my acceptance in the community and my self–construction as *okupa*. (The names I use for the members of the community, throughout this book, are pseudonymous.)

"This phrase came to me in the morning on waking. It refers to the previous day when, after I'd cooked lunch... three new motorcycles with three young men with red tee-shirts roared up. The path is navigable on foot, by motorbike and Land Rover only. I advised Joshua (who'd come back to the village last week after an absence of weeks) up at the tents and told Rebecca down at the spring where we wash our clothes. I kept to the forest paths but then took some wet washing as a prop and walked by them (Carla and Miguel were talking to them) by this time one was taking photos of the village and two were up at the tents. I spoke to them in English, refused to produce my identification – as I said my passport is property of the Queen of Great Britain and they (not being Custom's Officials) don't have the right to see it. Furthermore I said I was a journalist working for *The Scotsman* newspaper investigating human rights and would observe carefully what they were doing. This caused much inner hilarity among the members of the community – especially when I demanded to see not only one policeman's (*Forales* is their official title as the ancient laws of Navarre are called *Fueros*) badge but also his identity card and photo – still refusing to show mine. I also said that my father had fought against the Nazis and that only Nazis followed orders without thinking or taking responsibility. The policemen evaded the subject. I then turned my back and continued to hang up the washing – heart shaking. They left but not without discussion (staged for our benefit I believe) whether or not to call a patrol car and take me to Iruñea or not. This incident at once made me the darling of the community, made me feel much more committed as an *okupa* – in my recent interpretations I've written "we" not "they" and also gave me an unnerving experience (slight though it was) of the omnipresence of the State."

Excursus B: Dividing the Task: Housework and Genderplay

I found Kevin Hetherington's *New Age Travellers* interesting in the dis/similarity of his descriptions of "vanloads of uproarious humanity" to my experience in the community. He notes that a "rather conventional gendered division of labour prevails amongst many Travellers, with the women doing most of the work while men sit around 'strumming guitars' " (Hetherington/2000/84).

I am unclear about the nature of this 'work' (New Age Travellers being more sociological than ethnographic in description), as Hetherington lists "housework and childcare, but also vehicle maintenance, fuel and water collection, waste disposal and general repairs" (*ibid*). Some of these tasks fall into traditionally gendered categories but some do not. Even if the mechanics who "spend a week underneath a van" are usually male then as domestic duties are (hopefully) more frequent than vehicular repair this division would still hold.

This is an immediate difference with the community I studied. Certainly Miguel was most knowledgeable about the workings of the Land Rover and Rebecca the best breadmaker but everyone took turns at cooking, fetching water and chopping wood for fuel. In the ethnopoem "A Perfect Anarchist" which follows, Carla makes breakfast but Joshua cooks and Rebecca is building fences and taking willow cuttings to root. In this example of 'a typical day' it is a woman who is making music but this is accepted as people would often engage in activity not immediately recognisable as 'work'.

Massage, for example, was very important not simply as preventative medicine to keep muscles supple and avoid strain – when orthodox medicine was difficult to access – but also as a physical bonding between members of the community, an aid to *comunitas* (see Hetherington/2000/64) without which the community would not survive daily emotional wear and tear. As massage was often practised with both participants naked, it served to sublimate sexual tension and to protect the current sexual status quo – and to seduce and subvert it!

Whittling, an activity my grandfather's (WW1 soldier) generation were fond of, was also common, both for spoons and candlesticks for the house and kitchen and for gifts when community members went to visit family and friends. Homemade gifts like this, as well as subverting a "conventional gendered division of labour", (as when Pamela carved spoons or I did embroidery) complied with social expectations of gift-giving at Christmas or birthdays and also implicitly critiqued these feasts' increasing commercialisation. As for 'guitar strumming', when I played guitar in the evenings it was not only to entertain the community but to practise the songs I would use for busking – which would bring money into the community. The most parasitic activity going on in the community was probably my own dream analysis but even that became a recognised and valued skill which I shared and taught to others.

Thus analysis of the division of work in a community must first understand what 'work' is to that community and categories such as 'valued activity' and 'non-valued activity' may be more useful. Valued activity traditionally associated with males and with females was spread unevenly over the community – with most people engaged in most things but the inequality of skill was firstly viewed as a consequence of upbringing but secondly challenged as the non-traditional gender acquired the 'other' gender's skills and thirdly accepted pragmatically within the community ethos of variation of skills among members, all of which should be taught as far as possible to those interested. As an example: Dave knew most about using a treadle lathe for spoons and candlesticks whereas Rebecca knew most about constructing shelves with *macramé* and planks, this latent gendered division was broken down when both taught their skills to Pamela.

Hetherington assumes a bi-polar division of gender which transgender criticism finds oppressive. Shannon Bell states that "gender is a cult" (Bell/1993/111) and as I was typing up this dissertation during the World Cup (whose purpose can be read as a global performance of gender role-playing with massive participation at home), I began to agree. Do we find self-help (feminist or sexist) literature about men and women reassuring because they convince us that such simple beings actually exist? Kate Bornstein (playwright of *The Opposite Sex...Is Neither!*) is more forthright: "sex is fucking, everything else is gender" (cited in Bell/1993/104). Bell elucidates, explaining for me a negative reaction I had in the community when – to play the fool on an exceptionally tense occasion – Dave put on a tutu, showing off his muscular hairy legs and chest. I, who often wore the kilt, did not like it and now see my feeling as a resistance to the following:

"Every lesbian and gay man is transgressing gender roles and gender rules. Whereas not all transgendered people are lesbian and gay, all lesbians and gays are transgendered. (Bell/1993/116)"

Space does not permit a sociological comparison between the *okupa*/ libertarian self as perceived by the wider community in *Euzkal Herria*/ Spanish Territory and the public perception of "New Age travellers" in Heatherington's eponymous study. Suffice to say that his discussion of dirt, Bakhtin's carnivalesque and folk devils would illustrate much that I read in official Spanish media which is still fairly fascist.[35] An overlap between the two studies would have included discussion of the effect on Erkametza of the arrival of a Finnish young woman who identified herself negatively then positively as, "I'm not a punk ["anarco-punk" is a common designation among *okupa*s], if I defined myself I suppose I'd say I was a Rainbow Hippy."[36] I have included dream references to her and her Finnish male friend under the second stanza of the Erkametza poem, as he slept in a tent and she kept 'starry vigil'.

NOTES

[35] "pollution, while it is often represented in the form of dirt and filth, as is suggested by Mary Douglas' famous definition of dirt as 'matter out of place' is, in fact, a moral category that is expressed in symbolic form." (Heatherington/2000/21).

"The term 'folk devil' was introduced into sociology by Stan Cohen in 1972, in his now famous book *Folk Devils and Moral Panics*." (Heatherington/2000/54–57).

[36] See comment on Rainbow Fields Village (Heatherington/2000/73,78–9).

Chapter 6 Conscious and Unconscious Character Description:

i) Erkametza

To summarise the portrayal of members of the community, I first observe their appearance in the dreams then in the ANALYSIS taken as a whole, then discuss this with reference to our conscious relationship during my stay.

Carla is one of the four to be explicitly named in the dreams; the others are Dave, Ricardo and Xavier. This would either indicate that they were the most important to me and/or that I had more emotional conflict to work through with them. In the Dream 29 I focus on Carla's radical hairstyle, her relationship with a man in the community and (in Dream 31) her letting something fall. In the ANALYSIS I link her to my sister A1f, as organised and practical and earth-motherish. Carla inspired the whole poem, getting up early one morning after a hard day's manual labour to make bread and set out a magnificent breakfast. I have commented above (under Community) on how she avoided clashing with me over the subject of hierarchy. Carla and I had a relationship which was a complex one of mutual respect with a great sense of responsibility for the community on her part which placed her in a powerful position from which I attempted to bring her down. My sexual jealousy and her non-possessiveness further complicated my feelings for her. When I explained my interpretation of dream 31 to her and mentioned "*tu hombre*" (your man), she replied "*Yo no tengo hombre.*" (I don't have a man).

Dave in Dream 32 is preoccupied with food and shelter and in Dream 7a (where he is obliquely named) is red-haired and a good laugh. In the ANALYSIS I focus on his attractiveness and bring out my use of 'gay' Dave as an *alter ego* (obvious wish-fulfilment). He also appears as a hippy on the guru trail, and a musician. I describe my annoyance at his stubborn individuality, sympathy for him being unlucky in love and gratification at his recognition of my language skills mixed with my concern about interfering with community internal politics. Dave and I spoke English while alone, often massaged each other and shared a mad sense of humour. Despite being sometimes annoyed with him I enjoyed our friendship and tried to define it as something more intimate – a manipulation which he resisted but continued to be close.

Ricardo in Dream 32 is trapped and has to be rescued. The ANALYSIS portrays him as a philosopher and intelligent 'native informant' as well as bringing out our mutual cleansing, my phallic fixation with him and my inability on occasion to shut up and listen! His gardening is mentioned and his rather vigorous cooking techniques. Ricardo was at first the most important person for me in the community as I had known him previously in his incarnation as a philosopher and he was my 'in' and a close friend. For most of the first week we slept together in the tent until I went to Chinebro then moved into the house. I enjoyed cooking and this involved gathering herbs and vegetables from the plot where he was often working and we collaborated on digging a drain, which is mentioned in the poem. He was friendly and flirtatious but definitely 'straight'. It seems that our often watering the garden – and each other – was sublimating desires at least on my part which would have interfered with our friendship. I was also often tried to persuade him to take up studying again.

Xavier in Dream 11, the dream with most written in Spanish, will come to visit me. In the ANALYSIS (of Dream 4; Dream 11 I interestingly ignore completely) he is also an attractive man, a loner, a hard worker supportive of the community and someone who I managed to reach out and touch. The poem brings out his learning *Euskera* (Basque) and I picked up a smattering from him and others. At first I felt him a tough nut to crack then we seemed to suddenly become very close then, after I came back from Chinebro, (where Dream 11 was recorded and where initially he was going to go, with Rebecca) we were friendly but distant. I wondered if he didn't go to Chinebro because of me. I respected him and admired his hard work in labouring and learning. I have no idea what he thought of me.

Rebecca, Pamela, Pepe and Miguel are represented in the dreams (by over-determined figures or allusion) but not named. Rebecca is portrayed in the ANALYSIS as interested in Scottish culture and a great breadmaker. She also appears to be manipulated by the forces of political opposition to the community and to be emotionally both sensitive to the pain of others and needy. The overwhelming impression is of her passion for the freedom of the community. My scones and oven-door paranoia both being famous in the community,

I appreciated Rebecca's baking skills. The poem shows her taking willow-cuttings and building a fence and she was doing the latter when the *Forales* turned up and I advised her to hide. Her, typical, answer was that it cost her more to hide than to confront them. We had a warm relationship of sympathy with admiration on my part and I think amused tenderness on hers.

Pepe is mentioned in the ANALYSIS as part of my helpful networking (when he arrived at the end of the first week) and as inconveniently 'straight' and so interested in the women. I admired his mix of manliness and ability to do both manual and emotional work well and the poem reflects this. He was quite complimented and unperturbed by my attraction to him and our conscious relationship focussed more on meditation, group dynamics (it was he who instigated the consensus workshop) and our (and Dave's) interest in New Age beliefs. We were friendly and found each other interesting.

The ANALYSIS lumps Pamela together with Carla and Rebecca and focuses on her as 'German' and on my ambivalence about that. Romantic confusion is also mentioned and the poem sees her playing her flute, gazing out at her beloved and notes her 'dreaming' with 'magic mushrooms'. Pamela and I sometimes spoke English but we were both resistant to the epithet '*guiri*' (unlike Dave who didn't care) and tried to be as Iberian as possible. As she was taking an extended break from university it was with her that I most felt my dual identity. We were mutually jealous yet though we often drove each other mad (I being more irritated than she) she was the person I could speak most frankly to. My poetic vision of her as a siren alludes to my constantly trying to rescue someone from her and yet being drawn into listening to the sound of her loss. Between ourselves we had no power struggles or romantic feelings and she mostly felt like a sister. I think I felt to her like a slightly overbearing older brother who had to be sometimes heard and other times humoured if not flatly contradicted. With all these complications we were friendly and sometimes close.

Miguel also attracts me in the ANALYSIS which concentrates on his driving the *furgonetta* (van) to 'recycle' food from Iruñea (as does the poem). His commitment to anarchist principles is also mentioned – although the phrase may be ironic as a reference to his avoidance of the symposium over lunch on hierarchy. Miguel was the only *Eskaldun* (Basque) and that, together with his beauty, physical strength and unregenerate aggressive virility made me quite in awe of him at first. He also hardly spoke and I wondered if I was welcome. I discovered that he often talked about emotional problems to Dave and our moments of greatest intimacy were when, overhearing him doing this, I wordlessly (my voice lost for three days) embraced him; and when I accompanied him 'recycling' and as I unloaded the van of heavy Land Rover tyres he clapped me on the shoulder shouting "*¡Allí está! hermano Alan*" (That's it! brother Alan). I sublimated my attraction towards him into tenderness but we lost a hard-won closeness when I felt he'd stranded me in Iruñea and I got lost on the way back (in fact I could have stayed in the *Gatztetxe*). We continued to be cordial but I felt he wasn't good at emotional work (as I allude to in the poem) and we never moved on.

Joshua was back in Erkametza when I came back from Chinebro – so about half of the 'month' studied. Neither he nor Enrique (who was gone for most of the latter half) are even in the ANLAYSIS in more than an oblique way. I liked both of them, admired Joshua's cleanliness and order in the kitchen (which usually offended my Virgoan sensibilities) and would discuss Basque politics with him (which is why I have put ETA material under his stanza, not that he was a member), listening to Basque music while he was cooking in the peace he always managed to create. He liked to hear me sing and play the guitar and was very *cariñoso* (tender, caring – the word doesn't translate) towards me. I liked him and we had an uncomplicated friendship which is probably why he doesn't appear in the dreams.

The same is probably true of Enrique who was the best listener of the community and so a natural barman (as I mention in the poem). He was quite fascinated by my travelling and education and seemed to want a mentor. I wasn't sure about this but we only talked about that after this first month. Coincidentally (perhaps because I prioritised relationships which were more problematic), we didn't spend much time together in the first month but were always friendly.

The Finnish young man is mentioned in Dream 31 as alien and he and the young woman appear in the ANALYSIS under stanza two as beautiful, he singing and she off on a meditation course. They turned up in the last week and were immediately liked by everyone. Both were extremely attractive, she was a hippy and he a punk so they were very welcome. My overwhelming impressions were of their beauty and of how alien they were to me. She and I met up again in Barcelona when I went to see my girlfriend and he stayed in Erkametza. She also accompanied me when I went to Aoiz for the day and we talked a lot about New Age beliefs, of which she was a splendid example. Their relationship with me and with everyone was always positive (they both walked straight past the *Forales* – they turned up on that day) and I felt friendship and international camaraderie with them. As the ANALYSIS points out, by my positing them as alien, they probably made me feel more my kinship with the community.

ii) Chinebro

I stayed in Chinebro for ten days and Pancho, in the ANALYSIS gets unremitting bad press. He's portrayed as lazy, unwashed, untidy, unhygienic, careless of Chinebro which is in any case flea-ridden. All of this may have been true sometimes of Pancho and of Chinebro but also of Erkametza and the other villages, of the other *okupa*s and of myself. Why am I so negative towards him? The poem could not be more of a contrast and even the phrase "*aquí está todo para hacer*" (here everything remains to be done) is semi-ironic as someone said it to Pancho and he was annoyed about it. The poem was written in January '01 when I visited Chinebro with my girlfriend and Ricardo was also there. I was extremely happy, University was going well (so I thought!), my girlfriend and I felt we could work out our diverse paths together and Pancho and I became very close. I often took his side against Ricardo who I knew better and who tended to bully him. Suffice to say that by Autumn '02 all this had changed. I was struck by the fact that Pedro, a visitor who I got together with, was having a completely different experience and so was Pieter the Belgian who turned up for a while (like the Finns at Erkametza).

To summarise my own dream, ANALYSIS and poem *persona* is hardest of all. I feature in most of the dreams and will summarise who I am and what I'm doing so that the chronological development can be seen:

1 (Erkametza): uncertain identity/ judged by community

2 (Erkametza): organised academic/ male-bondingly playful/ discretely gay/ afraid of death.

3 (Erkametza): hospitable to guests/ caring for sick.

4 (Erkametza): insular Scottish/ informative/ affirmative.

5 (Erkametza): short-term visitor.

6 (Erkametza): occult/ energised/ magical/ bemused/ socially appropriate.

7 (Erkametza): friendly/ bourgeois/ appreciative of colours/ Scottish/ angry/ anti-academic/ helpful to differently-abled/ insecure about good deeds/ hospitable/ trusting/ anthropologist.

8 (Chinebro): seeking information/ sympathetic to American people

9 (Chinebro): regretful of earliness/ audience/appreciative of performance.

10 (Chinebro): tour guide / funny/ dancer/ interested/ sad about death/ excited about girlfriend/ anti-American terrorist/ suspicious/ insecure about being White/ not tent evangelist.

11 (Chinebro): chorister/ aristocratic page/ guitarist/ appreciative of singing/ suspect/ comic/ cosmopolitan/ expectant of visitor/ desirous of comforts of hotel/ voyeur/ critical of academic/ closet opener.

12 (Chinebro): upwardly mobile/ have flea in ear/ exiting student.

13 (Chinebro): preoccupied with hospitality/ robbed of rhythm/ martial artist/ afraid/ javelinist/ rescuer from wreck/ bad basketball player/ gay.

14 (Chinebro): pilgrim/ subterranean/ claustrophobic/ liking flowers/ searching for spiritual mentor/ religious postulant/ forgetful.

15 (Chinebro): inquisitive/ play-goer/ expecting tardiness/ giving sweet/ wear glasses.

16 (Chinebro): downwardly mobile/ asking for friends/ abetting cake thief/ jealous of friend's wife.

17 (Chinebro): son/ brother/ finds cat/ teacher/ surprised at old person coming/ helpful/ in company with drug users/ key worker/ unsure of rightness of action.

18 (Chinebro): sexually successful.

19 (Chinebro): wet/ tired/ wearing fake torn hat/ tired of introductions/ kin/ accepted/ part of it all.

20 (Chinebro): surprised at cleanliness/ unsure of gender due to hair/ worried about fleas/ informative about Finko/ planning complications /not comprehending not going straight/ university alumnus/ primary school alumnus/ discrete but incorrect translator/ waiting to eat/ brother (in-law to be)/ pacifier/ clear road blockage/ hurry to catch up/ guru devotee/ Scottish country dancer/ makes up dance.

21 (Erkametza): tidying up village/ unsure of motives/ unsure of support/ kidnapper/ *Ettara*/ sailor/ ..../ free-loader/ leaving domestic women/ hope kids not tiresome/ homicidal to attractive men/ look down on people/ late/ claiming kinship/ have private locked room.

22 (Erkametza): telepathic/ teacher/ remorseful at not helping woman/ pursued by spies/ martial/ reproved/ academic colleague.

23 (Erkametza): (No image of self.)

24 (Erkametza) husband/ diver/ rescuer/ searching for people/ take oxygen/ want illumination/ discussing need for illumination/ calling ash-covered animals to me/ patting them/ telling girl/ limiting own bodily damage/ wondering about animals getting in/ take out catamaran/ leave someone else's money/ don't listen to Ricardo/ need to go to London & go out in boats & discover truth.

25 (Erkametza) on university campus/ explaining mythology/ going to receive info on TV serial/ surprised at twins being Western/ receiving & sympathetic to unrequited love.

26 (Erkametza): name-tagging box/ prohibiting first years from using box/ providing means to wash/ explaining machines/ conflict about people going/ reading book.

27 (Erkametza): loved town/ regret damage to town/ former churchwomen's supporter/ discrete/ preoccupied about food (preparation).

28 (Erkametza): unwelcome sleeping quarters/ listening to Harry Potter tapes/ out disguising masked person/ leaving for far away.

29 (Erkametza): illuminate house/ receive aggression/ stupid cook/ funny/ eating light–bulb lollypop/ welcoming to *Etarras*.

30 (Erkametza): refusing to be stressed out/ wanting to buy/ resisting own racist prejudice/ victim/ preferring local asceticism.

31 (Erkametza): picking up fragile alien object/ crossing road/ unsure of religious denomination/ unsure of direction.

32 (Erkametza): rescuer/ preoccupied with food & shelter/ unconcerned with nuns/ wary of bulls/ opening gate/ brushing teeth/ receiving & questioning criticism from aunt.

It is difficult in such a cursory survey to appreciate the depth of the dream imagery, so I ask the reader not to give up and to actually read the appended dreams, poems and ANALYSIS and use this list as a mnemonic aid. A move from preoccupation with hospitality as a receptionist to the same concern as a member of the community can be seen. Pro/anti American sympathies seem not so much in movement as juxtaposed but there is definitely a movement towards identification with Basque nationalism. The critique of poor hygiene is constant but there is more and more identification with the community as time goes on.

Chapter 7 Monsters from the *Id*: Revenge, Racism, and *Erotica*.

The cross-referencing and over-determination of dream narrative meant that certain themes featured frequently. One about conflict with the Department, usually involving Harry Potter, was so pervasive that I seriously considered reversing my ethnographic focus from the community to the Department – in the spirit of that 'parochialising' which Gayatri Spivak calls for. I complained of this in a letter to my supervisor where I told him to try and resolve money matters (the promised financial support for fieldwork upkeep never arrived – hence the busking and hitching) so that I could stop dreaming about how angry I was with them! This conflict was often symbolised by the figure of Harry Potter who had become an important *persona* for me of winning against the odds, given the departmental powers stacked against me) as the discussion under Oneirocritical Methodology shows.

The negative portrayal of known persons in dreams for purposes of revenge or self–aggrandisement I have commented on above in discussion of Dream 2. Such portrayal must be read as subjective caricature. Racism and other prejudiced material are more difficult to deal with. If my dreams present a friend in a negative light, the astute reader will give the friend the benefit of the doubt. If I, as White, represent a Black person negatively then a White reader sharing un/conscious racist assumptions may let my racism by uncensored. Edgar comments on racist assumptions in identifying 'shadow' imagery:

"With regard to the example of racial stereotyping, Jung's analysis of the 'black man' as representing the 'shadow', or inferior, personality is now rightfully seen as racist by contemporary commentators on Jung's work." (Edgar/1994/52)

Dreams 17 and 30 portray Black men as drug takers and muggers. The former, as the ANALYSIS (17 xiii, under my stanza in the Erkametza poem) points out was quite normal in the (White) community so why did I need an image of a Black man? I am aware of this racism only in the ANALYSIS of Dream 17 but in Dream 30 itself I attempt not to be prejudiced – only to then create confirmation my fears. This racism is mitigated only slightly by my own, ambiguous, Black identity in Dream 1 in the ANALYSIS of which I consciously employ a technique of multiple allusion so as to have positive alternatives to the 'shadow' imagery. I have the same political motivation as Edgar but I see that White people are still generally racist, so if an image of a Black person is obviously functioning as a 'shadow' in a dream that dream will be misinterpreted if this function is ignored. However is there hope in this technique of conscious positive allusion and can it change the way White people dream? Could I better struggle with my own racism in Dream 30 because I had tried to 'de-program' my racist responses in Dreams 1 and 17? Is the Black man in Dream 30, as well as mugger and Harry Potter/ George Weasley also an angel (in Hebrew a 'messenger' – the consciousness of my own racism?) with whom, as Jacob, I struggle with/ embrace all night and who leaves me wounded and wiser?

"30(iv) A short story I wrote (after the very successful "Sun on Pale Skin" presentation to the Dept. and before the bitter parody – both based on Harry Potter) involved the "transmogrification" of Harry Potter from White to Black and George Weasley (who's White) putting his arm around Harry after dealing with the evil Draco Malfoy. This image is a reversal, the black guy embraces me (presuming that in the dream I'm White!)"

A very prominent theme was sexuality, and some of my dream analysis may well be an instance of what Llobrera entitles "*pornografía*". I can see what he means in the sex scene at the end of the ethnographic work "Shabono" by Florinda Donner (1982), a work which she interestingly describes as "a subjective account of the surplus data". Is that because she stood up from her folding table, left behind the hamper from Fortnum and Mason's and walked off into the forest with the Iticoteri clad in nothing but *onoto* paste and underpants and thus discovered what she never could have otherwise? James Clifford comments on this level of involvement:

"Only recently, and still rarely, has the taboo been broken (Rabinow 1977); (Cesara 1982). Why should sharing beds be a less appropriate source of fieldwork knowledge than sharing food?" (Clifford /1997/ 72)

Johnathan Culler (1997) notes that:

" 'schools' of literary criticism [tend]… to give particular kinds of answers to the question of what a work is ultimately 'about': 'the class struggle' (Marxism); the possibility of unifying experience (the New Criticism); 'Oedipal Conflict' (psychoanalysis)" (Culler/1997/64).

Employing a Freudian analysis one should not be surprised at so much sex! I could have used Jung but in my experience of Jungian dream interpretation everything ends up very beautiful and vaguely spiritual (but mostly just vague, which is why I didn't use him) The decision to include Dream 2 (the best example of classic Freudian forensic analysis) was a difficult one and I'm sure there was a reason why I did not remember my dreams of the night between Dreams 7 and 8. The sexual content of the dreams was more of a problem for me than for the members of the community who were very open to such discussion and were often complimented by having starred! This open attitude helped me to limit my censorship of the dreams to one instance each [Dream 21b & Dream 2 (iv/v)]. Not doing groupwork I did not face the problems with interpretation which Edgar notes:

"My gender in the research process was probably most manifest in the interviews with some female members when I felt less than confident in pursuing very emotive and intimate issues for them when they emerged. For instance when one female member referred to having "blue pencil"[37] dreams about other group members I didn't follow it up." (Edgar/1994/19)

I feel that the amount of self–revelation (even of unconscious impulses) should be up to each individual ethnographer but to cheerfully record Inuit avuncular initiatory *fellatio* or adolescent free-for-all in Western Samoa and then to pretend to the sexual stoicism of a mediaeval monk [38] is to risk the Malinowski syndrome. The real scandal of his 1914-1918 field diaries of Mailu and the Trobriands **[39]** was not their racism, homesickness and lust but the fact that his official ethnography bore no trace of this and so, to reverse Donner's description, pretended to be an objective account of the essential data.

NOTES

[37] "a [phallic] 'mini-archetype', to borrow Jung's term (1959:3), for the group." (Edgar/1994/13). "Especially if one thinks of the rubber on the tip!" David Fairbairn, in conversation, Stirling, Aug. '02

[38] For which, see Umberto Eco's *The Name of the Rose*!

[39] Pub. Posthumously in 1967, twenty-five years after the death of the author, as Llobrera notes (1990/53).

Chapter 8 Oneirocritical Methodology – a Shut Eye View.

Freud informs us that "in the later years of antiquity, Artemidorus of Daldis was regarded as the greatest authority on the interpretation of dreams, and the survival of his exhaustive work [Oneirocritica] must compensate us for the loss of the other writings on the same subject."[40] The 'oneirocritical' methodology I have been using for this ethnography came to me upon waking one morning in the Youth Hostel after a restful sleep in which the problems with the Department had receded to reveal bright hopes for my forthcoming fieldwork. *Contra* Edgar I use 'oneirocritical' with the full and open value of its long use and resist his attempt to replace it with the misnomer 'dreamwork':

"Hierognosis [Corbin 1966:384][41] refers to the hierarchical classification of the different orders of visionary knowledge displayed both in dreams and waking realities. Therefore dreams would be interpreted by oneirocritical means by reference to the status of religious imagery appearing in any dream." (Edgar/1994/43)

Dreams themselves are not simply outpourings of excess *libido* (as some psychologists view them) but also have a critical role. In Dream 10b mentions "...(a book) and the Dedication to Harry Potter." The accompanying note in the ANALYSIS (iv) has:

"it would be interesting to note what is written in the dedications of the Harry Potter books I have read (1–4). The folder which encloses these notes is of Harry Potter, which I bought in Tesco in Stirling in a fit of impishness as a member of the R.S. Dept. condemns it as "Capitalism" see note (vii) dream 26."

In the latter dream's ANALYSIS I now,

"wonder if the "dedication" is actually the motto of Hogwarts *"draco dormiens nunquam titillandos"* which is a version of "let sleeping dogs lie" but literally "never tickle sleeping dragons"." [Dream 26(vii)]

Having decided this to be so, I then apply this motto in the ANALYSIS of Dream 28(v):

"28(v) A short story I wrote about Harry Potter and "transmogrification" was based on an incident in the book (Book 3 I think) where he and Ron shapeshift into the form of the enemy (Draco Malfoy and his sidekick) to learn their secrets…("Draco" means "dragon" and thus the motto of Hogwarts would apply)…My conflict is whether to "let sleeping dogs lie" or to set them at each other's throats".

However what Dream 26 actually says is "Reading a book from Denise to Harry the dedication is confused." Its explanation [note (vii) of the ANALYSIS, quoted above] is misleading. The dedication of the book of the series I'd most recently read, Book 4: Harry Potter and the Goblet of Fire, is:

"To Peter Rowling, in memory of Mr Ridley and to Susan Sladden, who helped Harry out of his cupboard." (Rowlings/1990).

Given the amount of homoerotic reference in the dreams I obviously have a few candidates in mind to help out of the closet! Also, given the position of Harry in the Dursley household (forced to live in a cupboard under the stairs) Dream 28 also makes more sense:

"28(ii) On the eve of my departure to the Basque Country I pinned a satirical episode on the Religious Studies Students Board – it was immediately censored – describing my feelings at the shoddy treatment by the department and manifesting the support of Hermione (F and K. from Stirling and also my sister B1f.) and the power of magic."

Thus Dream 26 can be read as an attempt to jog my memory because there was an association I was not seeing. In fact I was only able to confirm this when back in Scotland. Freud sees the Super-Ego (as well as the *Id*) as unconscious (and Anna Freud even the Ego in its self-defences) so this critical, corrective faculty of dreams I would hope would serve to challenge the ethnographer when an

43

interpretation of the culture of a community was misconstrued. Although ambiguous, the unconscious is extremely perceptive. With all this evidence of my subconscious using dreams intelligently to try and communicate with my conscious mind, I cannot agree with Edgar in his chillingly rationalist and positivist conclusion:

"Symbols then, can be said to mean nothing except what is produced by the audience and the group interaction. If this thesis is correct then dreams do not represent the fundamental truths of the personality as psychoanalysis asserts. Rather they are formed through the bricolage process and their essential nonsense is made culturally meaningful solely through the group process. Such a perspective positions social anthropology, and perhaps sociology, in a powerful position to claim an increased role concerning the elucidation of the processes and outcomes of dream interpretation in modern society." (Edgar/1994/80)

This seems to be at odds with his own, previous, work [cited in Note 57] in which he observes:

"the impact of dream imagery on the dreamer, in this case the ethnographer, and the congruence of at least parts of the imagery with central preoccupations of the community in question" (*op cit/* 81).

What did I gain from employing oneirocritical methodology and what, if I were to expand this prolegomena into a fuller ethnography, would I do differently? The first bonus was acceptance. My willingness to be object of study reflected my academic gaze onto myself and though Llobrera complains that the "*problema del etnografía moderno, con su énfasis en el problema dialógico del encuentro entre sujeto y objeto, es su carácter narcisista.*"[42] this vision is 'warts and all'. To continue the metaphor: if I am gazing into the pool of my dreams to see my own face, I also see those of the community. In a "back to nature" type community such as this one, pre-industrial skills are greatly valued and, as noted above, being able to interpret dreams and share this skill gave me a valued place – especially (as in most communities) when rubbing along together needed more lubrication than the leaky Land Rover!

This acceptance was crucial in a community where vigilance in the order of the day, when day or night uniformed thugs can roar up to harass, beat up and arrest members of the community and destroy all their painstaking agricultural and artisanal labour and their very dwellings. The methodology enabled me to mitigate people's fears that the information might be misused, my dreambook was always lying about and several people read English and the native and near-native speakers could translate. People would ask me what I'd dreamed and be interested in my interpretations – often as a prelude to bringing up a dream of their own.

The second bonus was that, in the process of information-gathering, the dreams functioned as Tony Buzan's 'mind maps', or perhaps better, as the "link system" a mnemonic technique in which "you throw things together, place things on top of each other, or substitute one for the other". This description of a very similar process to Freudian dreamwork is combined with "outstandingness… the combined image must be larger than life, garishly coloured, humorous or absurd; and you must where possible, be able to imagine yourself tasting, touching, hearing, seeing and smelling it" (Buzan/1988/43,44). A good example of this is the Documentary Comic Book Series. I can easily recall information from *Freud for Beginners* but as for *Why Freud was Wrong* what sticks in my mind are precisely Freud's dream analyses because, unlike Webster's prose, they are so lively.

The dreams, written down upon first awakening, would stay in my mind during the day was well as being discussed with other people while we were working. In Dream 9, for example, the image of Rebecca as Coppelia making robotic movements yields the information about the *Billera* (meeting), its function and frequency, her worries about court action and decision to prioritise the latter. Further notes to this would have included the informal postal system [the lawyer's letter arrived in Aoiz – see Dream 24(xv) under Miguel – was driven and walked up to Erkametza by a friend of the community, whereupon it was relayed by shouting up the mountain to Rebecca, walking beside me to Chinebro] and the relationship of the community to a network of individual, helpful lawyers and social workers etc. who worked free of charge to help in the effort against the dam. This mnemonic excellence [43] of overdetermined dream images and their subsequent agglutination of material meant that the

45

use of the methodology freed most of the day to normal community life instead of time-consuming questionnaires,[44] interviews, 'counting things' and general anthropological head-measuring.

Finally oneirocritical methodology is aesthetically pleasing. The right/ left brain blend that it necessitates gives rise to poetry naturally and to jokes and puns of language, mythological allusion and stories upon stories. My Voudou teacher in the Institute of Culture and Creation Spirituality, Luisa Teish, said that Yourouba spirituality is like a circle, you have to go all the way round to know where you're starting from.[45] In the Department of Religious Studies, Stirling, I saw a piece of paper attempting to reduce the Yourouba pantheon to a diagram (most of it wrong, Exu always gets the last laugh!). The representation of another's culture is not only made richer by story, poem and dream: it is made possible.

For all my, qualified, admiration for Freud, it is obvious by his writings (and especially his dealing with colleagues) that he was autocratic. I believe that the critical part of my evaluation must be inspired, in contrast, by anarchists. Félix García Moriyon speaks of Bakunin's *Memorias de un Revolucionario* (Zero, Madrid 1973):

"Todo el esfuerzo teorético y practico del anarquismo estuvo a hacer compatibles la libertad y la solidaridad... las formulas organizativas que hicieron posible su ejecución practica siendo la autogestión y el contrato libre... En que media lo consiguieron, es algo difícil de valorar"[46]

and then quotes Kropotkin:

"empece a apreciar la diferencia que existe entre servirse del principio del mando y la disciplina o valerse del mutuo acuerdo. El primero es de gran efecto en un desfile militar; pero carece de valor allí donde se trata de la vida real, y solo se puede obtener el éxito por el esfuerzo supremo de muchas voluntades convergentes en un mismo fin."[47]

While my methodology, as I have noted above, did proceed with the helpful suggestions and information of the community and an explicit censorship which I was trusted to internalise, I could not say that it was undertaken with strictly anarchic principles. I confess to having been swayed by reading of the experiences of ethnographers who attempted to write ethnography-by-consensus and whose 'native informants' collaborating on the editing process 'turned it into mush'.[48] As I stated in the Community section, one justification for this could be the ethos of the community that, recognising the inequality of skills among the members, those with less know-how would simultaneously defer to those with more, while learning the skill and thus equalising the levels of ability. This is of course an ideal situation, (anarchist groups seem to have the ability to be at once extremely idealistic and to rub along with very botched circumstances and far from perfect people); individual people's abilities and inclinations to learn do not usually extend to all the skills necessary for the life of a community. However I wonder what would happen with more time, when the community was more *au fait* with Freudian dream analysis (which needs only a fairly forensic mind and an ability to spot bad puns).

I had participated in 'dream-groups' in ICCS (mostly Jungian–based) but did not attempt to start one in the community. The reasons why it did not occur to me were my desires both not to disrupt the normal life of the community (a fallacy since the addition of one to a group of ten is a big change) and also, aware of the suspicion of academia, to work discretely. This 'discretion' diminished as I shared more of my work but I at first wanted the people to get to know me rather than consider an abstract academic proposal sent by letter (which I feared they would refuse). As is apparent in the first dream, although Ricardo had vouched for me I was still wary of my perception by the community. More honesty and more trust (and possibly more patience as to starting-time) may have dissolved that apprehension.

Edgar's more participatory role [49] as "dreamwork facilitator and resource person for a, more or less, autonomous group." (Edgar/1994/1) was neither autocratic nor anarchic but democratic and encountered the problems with representing the majority and quashing of the minority that democracy always will:

"Four main areas of conflict emerged in the dreamwork groups studied. These were the nature of dream interpretation; the nature of the group; the role of myself as facilitator; dealing with the evidently

47

'different' orientation of one of the group members."
(Edgar/1994/35)

The 'nature of dream interpretation' seems fairly pre-determined:

"The analysis proper proceeds in four stages.
The first is concerned with "dreamwork", the way that the narration to and within the group can be shown to be collectively converted into a verbally expressed narrative of an experience seen as having hitherto been concealed and confined to the imagination." Second, I turn to the analysis of structure and process in the group itself and the communicative context in which this dreamwork took place.

Third, I use a hermeneutic analysis to unpick the emic and etic interpretive, and to some degree feminist-inspired, perspectives used by the group to make sense of the narratives they have collectively created.

Finally, I move outwards to the processual, meaning-creating and outcome, analysis of such groupwork methods as gestalt, psychodrama and imagework which are used to elicit meaning from narrated dream imagery.

I conclude that dreams are transformations of cultural symbols and that their interpretation is an example of what Obeyesekere,[50] significantly calling on both psychoanalysis and cultural analysis, has called 'the work of culture'." (Edgar/1994/1)

Even so, there is considerable variation in "the range of interpretive schemata within which group members explored, explained and understood their reported dreams" (Edgar/1994/43):

"the approaches used included quasi-religious, Freudian, Jungian, revised psychoanalytic, gestalt, transpersonal and what I define as a socio-political contextualisation approach emanating from a structuralist perspective." (*ibid*)

Edgar gives an informative survey of "historical development of dream theory" (*op cit*/5) and does not find any other instances of oneirocritical methodology apart from his own, previous work (which he appends).[51] His comments on the geographical limitation of anthropological interest in dreams invite postcolonial analysis:

"Whilst anthropology has in the past only considered the dreams of bounded groups in the third world as of cultural significance, my thesis asserts the significance of dream and its elucidation in modern society as a vital source of understanding and information about the culturally constituted and becoming self." (*op cit*/80)

"it is perhaps somewhat novel for the study of dreaming, dream narration and dream interpretation in the western industrialised world to be the ethnographic focus, although the work of Hillman is similarly focused on the US context (1989:117–141)" (Edgar/1994/20)[52]

"Maggie has been marked from early childhood as the one to inherit her mother's altar and, along with it, the responsibility of serving the family spirits. Prescient dreams, starting when she was quite young, indicated that the spirits favoured her. Alourdes also had such dreams, beginning when she was little more than a toddler. For both of them, dreams continue to be significant life events, sometimes diagnosing current situations and sometimes foretelling important future events." (McCarthy Brown/ 1991/ 295, 296)

I juxtapose these quotations and wonder at my initial urge to use McCarthy Brown's work (with a mostly poor, Haitian diasporian community in Brooklyn) as instance of "third world" (would it not be 'fourth'?) and my own work (with a mostly nouveau–poor Western European neo-pastoral community up the Pyrenees) as set "in the western industrialised world"!

NOTES

[40] Ch.1 "The Scientific Literature on Dreams" of Freud/1888/60. Book title added by Freud's Editor.
[41] Corbin, H. (1966) "The Visionary Dream in Islamic Spirituality." In G.Von Grunebaum & R. Callois (Eds.) *The Dream in Human Societies*. Berkeley. University of California Press.

[42] "problem of the modern ethnographer, with their excessive emphasis on the dialogic problem of the encounter between subject and object, is their narcissistic character." (Llobrera/1990/47)

[43] See discussion above, on Harry Potter and dream memory.

[44] My supervisor wondered what the result would have been had I sent questionnaires. I laughed out loud as I imagined the examples of Dadaist artwork I may have received in response!

[45] ICCS is now The Sophia Centre, California. Louisa Teish is the author of *Jambalaya* (1986) London. HarperCollins. I paraphrase her words from class, Autumn 1990.

[46] "All the theoretical and practical effort of anarchism was poured out to make compatible liberty and solidarity... the organisational formulas which make possible its practical execution, being self-management and free contract...in what measure this was realised, is rather difficult to evaluate". (García Moriyon/1992/195)

[47] "I started to appreciate the difference that exists between making use of the principal of command and discipline or preferring mutual accord. The first is of great effect in a military parade; but of no value when it comes to real life, and one can only obtain success by the supreme force of many wills converging on a single end...Kropotkin: 1973-A p.185)" (*ibid*)

[48] I confess to amnesia over the reference, I vaguely remember a Southwestern community in the U.S.A. in a book on issues in ethnography such as Agar (1996) or Marcus (1998).

[49] Although he and his colleague "usually did not work on our own dreams in the group" (Edgar/1994/38)

[50] Obeyesekere, G. (1990) *The Work of Culture.* Chicago, University of Chicago Press.

[51] Dreaming as Ethnography; paper given at the 1989 ASA annual conference: 'Anthropology and Autobiography.'

[52] Hillman, D. (1989) "Dreamwork and Fieldwork: Linking Cultural Anthropology and the Current Dreamwork Movement." In M.Ullman & C. Limmer (Eds.) *The Variety of Dream Experience.* Wellingborough: Aquarian Press.

Chapter 9 Conclusion

I have established that anthropology and especially ethnography (not to confuse them) is changing, turning towards postcolonialism. I have tried to follow that turn by steering clear of "Mediterranean" stereotypes while working in Spanish Territory. I have also celebrated the de-bunking of much anthropological imperialism masquerading as positivism. I have been inspired by the vulnerability of many recent ethnographers and the complexity of their reporting of fieldwork and used a delicately nuanced theory of 'self' to understand their work and mine.

In an excursus I have seen the bi-polar division of gender as oppressive and that of work/ non-work as inadequate. In my methodology I have displayed sensitivity to political and social concerns of the community studied and found in Freud a dream detective who (despite much-needed critiques)[53] remains useful today. I have foregrounded my unconscious portrayals of members of the community and our relations in order to challenge a false objectivity and to be aware of my effect on the system observed. Finally, as always in my two years at Stirling University, I have used a holistic mode of presentation, combining dream, poem and theory to prove the validity of oneirocritical methodology for self-aware ethnographers.

NOTES

[53] And the social devastation wrought by the 'Recovered Memory Movement's (mis)use of his work. See *Fredrick Crews and his critics* (1995).

Appendix A: Dreams

i) Dreams, Analyses and Comments discussed in this book

As explained above, the appended dreams and interpretation illustrate both ethnographic information and my perspective on my integration into the community. Basque names were chosen for most places and because of the need for anonymity names of people in the community are completely arbitrary – but in one case a dream played upon the new name and that of an old friend (the only name I do not change – with his permission).[54] Other names (unless famous and fair game or friars with pseudonyms already or unidentifiable) I have simply replaced with random letters of the alphabet. I indicate those names which are repeated by numbering the letters. The dissertation is lengthy due to translation. I am technically allowed to simply write in Spanish, but for greater ease of comprehension I translate into English. All translation is my own.

To simplify and reduce the bulk of the material, I underline what was originally written in Spanish/Basque/ etc. (noting, below, which) and indicate in the "ANALYSIS" what of the material following is of my mental association. "COMMENTS" are written directly upon waking – as (mostly) are dreams – and Freud included material of this type in the manifest content of the dream and not in the latent content. I feel this is because the ego defences [55] are still at work and the rational functioning of the brain is still too weak to overcome them (even though, contrarily, rationality also forms part of the ego defences). I started to write these in the beginning in order to remember associations which came to mind upon writing the dream but soon saw that I would have an overwhelming amount of material and much repetition. Those which I wrote I include here and note contemporaneously with the dream material itself in the analysis. This last is made up of free association and reflection upon word-play etc. which in English we refer to as "Freudian slips".

I recorded thirty-two dreams from the 18th September '01 till 20th October '01.[56] Freud interpreted "propinquity in time as representing connection in subject-matter" and so saw that as "one of a series of dreams" was "surrounded by the others it must have dealt with the same subject."[57] Therefore I count all dreams in the same night as one but use letters to differentiate them. The total word count for the dreams themselves is about 8,000 plus a further 13,000 for analysis. This is unsurprising as in the above –mentioned dream of "Irma" the dream sequence consists only of almost a page whereas the analysis extends to over fifteen. (Freud/1888/182–199) Freud uses such lengthy analyses not only to fully illustrate his method of the reversal of the aforenoted dreamwork processes.

In a compromise between space and verifiability, I include all the dreams recorded leaving intact the inserted numbers relating to the ANALYSIS, of which I use some that illustrate my perspective on the community and myself. The dreams seem to show a progressive identification (notwithstanding a counter-current of repugnance) with the community. In the first dream, which I compare with one of three weeks later, this is symbolised by a semi-circle (where my position *vis-à-vis* the group is one of aspiration) and then a complete circle (membership).

NOTES

[54] See Dream 7a, notes (i) and (iv) under Dave's stanza, Erkametza poem, below.

[55] See Osbourne (1993/147) on Anna Freud and Ego Defences.

[56] I chose this initial period as I was continuously in Erkametza or Chinebro and the dreams most highlighted my integration.

[57] All three quotes from Freud/1888/346. Each numbered dream, therefore, is a different night while letters refer to chronological priority and bracketed roman numerals to the notes of the ANALYSIS.

DREAM 1 Tuesday 18th September 2001 Erkametza [58]

I'm black (i). I'm in front of a circle of people judging me (ii) – semi circle like the nine or ten of cups (iii) – life in the countryside, *joie de vivre* (iv). There's a question – I can either be this and have that or that and have this (v).

COMMENT 1
Last night Ricardo and I talked about materialists and idealists in conflict – about the *okupa* village [59] and the dam. Yesterday we also discussed the emotional/sexual relations of the village and people's sexuality. The Jack of Spades – card I found on floor + turned over when stepped across threshold of Azarra. Overseer, observer, spy. Fears of that perception. We are 9 in the village – with me, 10 with the new guy (then I won't be the new guy). If 10 + me, 11, Jack (Page) of Cups – or Master like I wanted yesterday – proposal (of love).

ANALYSIS 1
1(i) Spanish. ASSOC: black sheep/ shadow/ beginning (Sweet Honey in the Rock Song, "If Black is the Beginning we will be forever.")

1(ii) I practise Capoeira, a Brazilian martial art created by Black people escaping slavery. We play/fight in a closed circle, a semi-circle means that we're putting on a demonstration – the onlookers are not part of the group.

1(iii) As in the Comment: there are eight in the village. As for the village, I have changed their names: Ricardo; Carla; Miguel; Rebecca; Dave; Pamela; Xavier and Enrique.[60]

I make nine and with the young man (everyone except me is between twenty and thirty) who arrives next week, Pepe, there will be ten of us. 1(iv) The tarot card, Nine of Cups, shows (in the Ryder-Waite version) a man standing before nine cups in a semi-circle and the meaning is indeed *joie de vivre/ bon viveur*. The ten shows a man and a woman embracing under a rainbow of ten cups which signifies domestic bliss/country life/tranquillity. In the Comment I add that if ten are facing me then the full number is eleven which in tarot would be the Page (Jack), in Spanish "*Soto*". Walking to Erkametza the previous day, I missed the way and ended up at Azarra, another *okupa* village where, stepping over the threshold, I saw a card face down which was the Jack of Spades/ *Soto de Espadas*/ Page of Swords – the Spanish playing cards are "swords", "clubs", "cups", and "coins/ gold" the meaning of which I comment on and refer to the saying "Jack of all trades and Master of none" about which I had a discussion with the community at Azarra, praising their workmanship. Obviously the phrase also describes my preoccupation with my extremely varied CV and the outcome of this dissertation for a Master of Philosophy degree.

1(v) This identity choice is very open to interpretation – sexuality, philosophy, cultural/ national etc. with benefits attached.

NOTES

[58] "Erkametza" is the *Euskera* (Basque) word for the oak which grows in abundance around the village. By coincidence, changing one consonant gives "Elkametza" which means "collective dream". I have included all the analysis written at the time to illustrate my method. In future dreams I only use appropriate sections.

[59] In the ANALYSIS I usually refer to the community as "the village" and Chinebro and the other villages by name.

[60] As noted in Dream 26(iii), Joshua came back. Counting Pepe and I, this brought the numbers to eleven.

DREAM 19 Sunday 7th Oct '01 Chinebro

Wet and tired, I arrived at the village (i). I'm wearing a "*Condes de Cuba*" straw hat (fake) and it's all torn (ii). I meet a plump girl who's sitting in a circle (iii) and I meet the others but I'm too tired and there's no time to do proper introductions (iv). When I leave I find out that the girl's mother is from Stanford-le-Hope like mine (v), that a guy (Am./ B1m.) is Scottish, wears a kilt and a white string vest and is stocky and has a beard (vi) and other coincidences. I feel very much accepted and part of it all now (vii).

ANALYSIS 19

19(i) In fact I did arrive thus the night of dream 5. I'm anticipating my arrival of Erkametza or consoling myself that all difficult situations come to an end.

19(ii) The previous night I and Pancho had annoyed each other – he being as disgusting and unhygienic as possible and I being as prissy. I'd considered whether to take the "Counts of Cuba" fake straw hat with me as it may have looked too bourgeois (which is what Pancho accused me of being.) In fact that is not only false but the veneer I have acquired is breaking down.

19(iii) Reminiscent of dream 1 but a circle now, not a semi-circle; i.e., in Capoeira terms, not a performance but training/ the real thing.

19(iv) Males and females kiss on the mouth in the *okupa* villages [see dream 9(x)]. I always feel that leaving and arriving in Latin cultures takes so much time: i.e. I'm anxious to be gone from Chinebro.

19(v) My sister A1f. is not as slim as my sister B1f. The circle may also be the Zodiac – my sister A1f. is Virgo – plumpness can be a symbol of good living and fecundity. Virgo is the Earth mother and noted for practicality and cleanliness. A feminist astrology book I read noted that it's the only symbol of a zodiac sign which has to be female and maybe that's why it gets such bad press (see my self-description as "prissy" in the last dream [Dream 18]). I often justify my cleanliness using the sign – to avoid offending people.

19(vi) The name [61] and description are as Scottish as can be and conjure up images of Scots Porridge Oats and the Highland Games of childhood. Tossing the caber? Wild oats? A joke in a play I performed in "that's not wild oats that's shredded wheat!"

19(vii) Not in Chinebro I don't but I do in Erkametza.

The contrast between the latent and manifest content of both dreams is interesting. Freud privileges the former over the latter but given the present post-modern fashion of 'surface is depth' there is no need to do so: they each reveal different takes on reality, one as valid as the other. The image-conscious censorship involved in the dreamwork process is just as much part of my identity as the iconoclastic rationality of analysis or the urges of the *id*-bent dream-thoughts. The manifest content of Dream 1 shows both a paranoia and an extreme desire for the bucolic as well as a dilemma of identity: the latent content is much more assured and presents the scene as display of martial art rather than court martial. As well as the Comment's more realistic view of life in the countryside, it is interesting in that it has a midway position (written upon waking it tries to analyse but also takes part in secondary revision) which sees the dreamer not as prisoner in the dock but as 'new boy'. A prisoner can expect to be condemned or acquitted: a new boy can expect an acceptance or rejection which is more gradual and less extreme. Even when the Analysis feature the word 'spy' it is only one of multiple meanings of the playing card and the focus is more on anxiety (not now paranoia) and aspiration to mastery in work.

In contrast, Dream 19 has a manifest content of welcome and unexpected kinship after an alienating and wretched experience but the latent content reveals more ambiguity. Even so, as in the previous dream, there are elements which can be read against the grain of both. The last sentence of the MC **[62]** is reassuring but this acceptance is only felt on leaving which could implicitly criticise the haste in the omission of formal introductions, delaying deeper acquaintance. Thus the judgement expressed against Pancho can be mitigated by the self-critique that if the dreamer conformed to the *mores* of the community there would be more chance of both accepting and being accepted as kin. The ten days in Chinebro were a watershed not only because of the increased level of responsibility I had but also because it was there that I was first identified as an insider [see Dream 14(xiv) under the ethnopoem of Chinebro, below].

NOTES

[61] The first combination "A" is the name of the MSP for Lifelong Learning whose remit takes in universities. This was consciously unknown to me at the time of dreaming and analysis but is indeed "a coincidence" because it is to him that I have taken my complaints about the Department. This kind of synchronicity, a more Jungian view of the Collective Unconsciousness, is outside the scope of this study. See Edgar (1994/9) "Freud usually related dream imagery to the past whereas Jung saw such imagery as possible symbolic sketches of the dreamer's future."

[62] I will use MC for manifest content and LC for latent content for the sake of brevity.

The dreams often display internal reference, as noted in 19(i). The dream (above) refers to:

DREAM 5 Saturday, 22nd Sept. '01 Erkametza

The manager of the Youth Hostel says to me and a girl "It's good to stay here for a few days and then go away then come back again."

COMMENT 5

Last night I hitched in a storm and got lost in the wood and arrived soaked and covered in mud because Miguel and Carla told me I couldn't come up (from Iruñea) in the Land Rover. I suppose the dream shows negativity and a desire to leave for a while – Youth Hostel – in Stirling and Granada that I'd thought of visiting.

ANALYSIS 5

I don't feel I can improve on the "comment" except to say that Cm. (the Scottish manager of the Youth Hostel,[…]) often goes away to […] to visit his girlfriend and this could indicate a desire to go to Barcelona to see mine. The previous day I had busked (in my kilt) in Iruñea and felt pleased with the monetary and conversational result and exhilarated and confused at being in the town after the peace of the country. When I visited the villages in January one girl made a remark that she felt people were spending too much time going down to Iruñea and not enough in the villages.

The condensation and over-determination operating in the dreams problematise their easy classification into groups, as does the mix of previous and present relationships and ethnographic information. The ANALYSIS of Dream 2a illustrates this:

DREAM 2 Wednesday 19th September '01 Erkametza

DREAM 2a: I meet Dm. (i) and ask him about his dissertation – he shows me a bunch of blank pages and I tell him to get on with it (ii). I pick up a water pistol (iii) and scoosh some guy coming downstairs – he did me before (iv). He runs after me and I open a door as if I'd run through but run into a girl's bedroom instead. He comes to the door. (v)

ANALYSIS 2

2a(i) Freud notes [63] that the appearance of known persons in dreams is often complimentary to the dreamer and can be an exaggeration or falsification of their usual actions and character, (see the other doctors in the dream about Irma's mouth). "Dm." seems to be a projection of my undisciplined Id, as "Em." in later dreams may be of my controlling Super-Ego and "C1f." (Stirling) and "Df." represent supportive, good, academics and friends. My sister B1f. also, often plays this latter rôle.

2a(ii) I hadn't yet interpreted the previous day's dream and so feel lazy.

2a(iii) Although this can be seen as phallic interplay, the association with waterpistols is of a handsome young Australian friend of a teacher in an English school I was managing with whom I agreed to trade board and lodging for some help with sports for the kids. His presence on Campus was problematic and I bent the Company rules but his contribution was praised by all. I feel that rather than an attraction to Dm., the association is to a desire to not be lazy (although conformist) but to excel and be praised even from an unusual position. This could apply both to the Dept. of Religious Studies at Stirling and to the Anarchist community here.

2a(iv) Another connection with the community is that Ricardo and I took showers down at the vegetable plot the previous day – there are two of them of about ten and seven sq. metres – using a hose, which Ricardo held for me then I poured buckets of water over him. The water source is a natural spring and all water has to be carried uphill to the kitchen (a roofed Sacristy of a roofless church) a five minute walk. Connections to the Youth Hostel in Stirling is that Fm., a close, Canadian friend, and I often took showers in adjacent cubicles and squirted (scooshed in Scots) each other.

2a(v) The end of the dream seems more clearly homoerotic with play on being "chased" and male/female rôles.

So shower frolics/ water pistol fights/ phallic interplay/ anarchist mutual aid in bathing and watering the kitchen garden.[64] "Dm." is a caricature, because the scene, 2a(ii), is an exaggeration of my meeting him at University and him telling me that he had to get on with his dissertation and felt behind (who doesn't!) in fact, in the ANALYSIS, note 2a(ii) admits that the judgement is displaced.[65]

The Analysis goes on to more ethnographic information about the community which I have included in the appropriate sections under the ethnopoem of Erkametza, below. Dream 2b continues the homoeroticism (for ANALYSIS see under Miguel in Erkametza poem, below) of 2a and the third dream of the series further complicates the sexual theme (ANALYSIS 2 below Dream 2c):

DREAM 2b: Walking after a prince, admiring him from behind – he looks like Gm. but is English (i). He phones his boyfriend to meet him in a pub but we're going to the restaurant where his boyfriend works – we could have met there but perhaps it would be indiscrete. (ii)

DREAM 2c: A man tells me his son (i) is watching T.V. (ii) in his room. I open the door and try to switch on the light (iii) but it doesn't work. I see a big bundle (iv) like a body in bed – I think he's dead. I'm afraid and I get out of the window and down a drain pipe (v) into a yard – like the *Frontón* (vi) in the *Gaztetxe* (vii). I think he look out the window (ix).

ANALYSIS 2
2c(ii) 'T.V.:' I usually translate as "transvestite" and could refer to my kilt (which is a play on words in Scots for "killed").[66]

2c(iii) The non-functioning of the light (consciousness), betokens something more obscure than in the previous note.[67]

2c(iv) So far almost all of the written description of the dreams has been in English but when I wrote the word "bundle" it was a translation of "*bulto*" (Spanish) meaning a hunched shape like a vulture.[68] A baby is often referred to as a "bundle" but this is a dead body. A few months ago [   ] died and I saw her minutes after, she was the same age as my father and we went to the cemetery together.[69]

2c(v) "Drainpipe" signifies for me the style of trousers my father always made all through the Seventies (he was a tailor) until we persuaded him to change – and thus "tailor-made".

2c(vi) If "yard" is graveyard then a list of associations links drainpipe with shroud/coffin: tailor-made / inside leg measurement (which I explained to a couple in the Youth Hostel when they needed measuring tapes for their Hotel uniforms)/ undertaker. If drainpipe can also refer back to part (1) as water carrier / pistol / phallus / hosepipe / then the "girl's bedroom" could be [   ]'s – the only one I've been in recently. Thus the guy chasing me in (1), as the son in (3), is Death: *Eros* and *Thanatos*.

NOTES

[63] See Note 65.

[64] See 'Erkametza' stanza on Ricardo who established the lower kitchen garden and usually was the one to water it, the poem refers to this.

[65] See Freud's dream "revenge" on his friend Dr. M to cover his own guilt about Irma not making full recovery. (Freud/1888/191)

[66] Traditional Iberian culture tends to reads "*la falda escocesa*" ("the Scottish skirt") as transvestism.

[67] In fact the ANALYSIS is trying to obscure Freudian references to *fellatio* and *necrophilia*.

[68] "*bulto*" means "1 bulk; lump 2 bundle; package 3 shadowy object" *Signet Diccionario*. The association is with Freud's "Art and Literature" (1988/209,172,184,185) linking Leonardo da Vinci's childhood dream of a vulture's tail in his mouth with the Egyptian phallic vulture goddess (*cf* Dream 25) Mut, and *fellatio*.

[69] This is perhaps a permitted allusion as the nurses had not closed her mouth and the vulture is a bird of death but it hides an urban myth I'd heard of a man in Stirling taking sexual advantage of cadavers and thus perhaps a shameful wish (hence all the obscurity) on my part to do the same with Ricardo while he 'slept as the dead'. I'd once characterised his repressed emotions as a "dam", *cf* note 2c(ix) under Chinebro poem.

The continuation of the ANALYSIS of Dream 2 (at the end of all this murky desire) is vital background to the community's legal situation, included under the ethnopoem of Chinebro, below. Having demonstrated the considerable detail involved in Freudian dream analysis I will now concentrate solely on the material in the ANALYSIS immediately pertinent to my perception of the community. Space does not permit the inclusion of the material on other associations which focus on my life back in Scotland, on family, friends, lovers, jobs and previous travels. However now, for reference I insert the full text of the other dreams.

DREAM 3 Thursday 20th Sept. '01 Erkametza

In the Youth Hostel (i), an Australian girl (ii) checks in and she wants her laundry done but I don't take the money yet (iii). Her companion – male – is sick and goes to bed. I go to the toilet and showers and open the doors to find a S. African rugby team there. They are all joking about something (iv). I go to see Alf., my sister, and we and a little girl – not Ef. (v) – leave the house. I've forgotten some books and a blanket (vi) but it's fine, I've got enough. Alf. was going to use her mobile phone to undo the alarm/lock (vii) so I could get in. Back at the Youth Hostel I go to the restaurant (viii) (I've never been there) to look for that guy who's sick (ix) and check on the laundry. I find two girls they don't know where he is and I don't know who they are – Australian or not.(x)

DREAM 4 Friday, 21st Sept. '01 Erkametza

Me and a guy or girl are on an island in the middle of the Forth Road Bridge (i) – which keeps the structure up (ii) and an Australian girl (iii) turns up and says, "Is this an island?" (iv) We say "Yes" and she leaves – going South. (v)

DREAM 6 Sunday 23rd September '01 Erkametza

DREAM 6a: I go into an occult temple, at street level, I look at all the Egyptian symbols and tarot cards (i) around the walls like Stations of the Cross (ii). I walk around to the left and suddenly lots of doors open on lighted rooms with people in them (iii), I say,

"Wow! I've never felt such a sense of magic!" As I say the last word, they say "energy" but I say "magic" and smile. I think that an older man is going to talk with me but instead an older woman does. She says "You and I are the North Pole (iv) and that is the South Pole" she refers to a magical machine that looks like a Van der Graaf generator (v). I have no idea what's going on (vi) so I just try to be open.

DREAM 6b: I'm on the bus with an older man from the temple and I want him to explain things but if he does he'll need to pay a return fare. I get off. (i)

DREAM 6c: I'm in an old people's home an old man gets up off his chair, tries to dance and collapses. Then he gets up and he's okay. (i) I'm in a car with a kid who's driving (ii) but they manage to stop before we hit a wall. Inside, I go for a pee in the most exquisite bathroom – the toilet is disguised – like a pretty commode (iii). A drunk old man and a big fat girl and a couple of others come in and I try to get them out of the room before they wreck it – it's the most expensive room/suite in the hotel. I want the old man to sleep in my bed in the same room as his son – as I'm going to sleep somewhere else –but he's so drunk he doesn't understand me. (iv)

DREAM 7 Monday 24th September '01 Erkametza

DREAM 7a: At home. We decide to go out. Dave **[70]** (i) meets a guy who later he tells me is annoying but I greet him in a friendly manner. The guy wears a grey floppy jumper which comes over his hands like the yahs in St.Andrews (ii). We – there's a girl too – I think C1f., go to a coffee shop (iii). I know it very well and like it very much but we sit in a grey area. I want to move but Dave explains that we're waiting for the guy (grey jumper) as he went for cash for Dave. Dave starts chatting up the waiter who's red –haired and a good laugh. He seems more interested than I thought he would be. (iv) Grey jumper arrives as Dave is ordering – whisky – hot chocolate with whipped cream etc. (v) I go upstairs and pass a bowl of angelfish/sea anenomies which change colour and move about slowly and beautifully (vi). Downstairs Dave had taken off one of his kilts (vii) and I thought it was mine (viii) and I almost hit him with it as I was so angry but it was his – much lighter. A waitress goes past and I leave the bowl of fish creatures and go to a table. All three are there but a man – some University type – is annoyingly reading the paper (vii) so I can't sit opposite them so we all sit on the same side. Later, in a van, we all go down a street where some mentally handicapped kids (viii) are playing and rehearsing a song. I'd commented earlier that that was the winner for next year's competition but now a girl – one of them – has lost her square plastic inflatable ball and I lean out the window of the van, pick it up and give it to her, wishing her luck. I think Dave will sneer but he doesn't. Driving back to the flats I hear Scottish Ceilidh music and everyone outside – old and young, tapping their heels (ix).

DREAM 7b: A2f. (i) from Cumbernauld is in my house – in [home town] – she goes out to talk to someone who's stopped in a car outside. She brings her back – she's an American girl who's waiting for the neighbours across the road to come back – she's visiting them. I say she can stay and try to make her feel at home as she waits. Meanwhile I'm thinking about kinship and trust. (ii)

NOTES

[70] There are two "Daves" in Dream 7 as the ANALYSIS tries to make clear: "7a(i) "Dave" is not he of this village but a flamboyant gay friend from Stirling University." The other is the "red-haired waiter". This is the only instance where the dreamwork plays with the fictitious names of the members of the community.

Tuesday 25th Sept. '01 Erkametza
No dream recorded.

DREAM 8 Wednesday, 26th Sept. '01 Chinebro

I go out in the streets, I think it's Edinburgh, there's a big crowd (i) – a group of young people passes me – I'm trying to get somewhere (ii) and so are they, they joke about going by skateboard/ (iii) plastic (iv). A woman who runs a hairdressers checks herself in the mirror before opening the door to a young man who explains that he doesn't have anything wrong with his hair [lice (v) for example] but it's too frizzy and full of electricity (vi), she nods and starts to help him. There's a great shop full of helpful people (vii) – now that the owners are away – I tell Capoeira B2f. (viii) about it and we go there. They give us information and things for free. As I walk back through the town I see American cadets stand to attention by their flag and I feel sorry for them (ix). Mum is having tea somewhere with a group of senior citizens. They are very appreciative of life. (x)

DREAM 9 Thursday, 27th Sept. '01 Chinebro

Hm. (i) and I in the early morning take a walk along to the Sea Life Centre in St. Andrews. (ii) There's mist and it's chilly. As we sit on the boardwalk (iii) a man, Im. (iv) from Granada, comes along and puts on angel wings and disappears. Another man, very funny and camp, comes along and puts on devil wings (v) he's wearing red tights (vi) he comes up and says Hello to Hm. We're inside and watching the spectacle of the pantomime (vii). I think, "What a pity it's so early (viii), more people could have enjoyed it but they seem to be enjoying themselves (the actors). One actress is Rebecca from Erkametza and she's acting like a robot (ix) – drinking tea etc. in a jerky manner. Hm. goes up and greets an old friend from Brazil (x) who's in the audience or acting – right in the middle of the performance – he ignores his supervisor who's sitting there quietly on the side with grey hair (xi). The director of the show says to Hm. (he's someone else now) "What do you think?" I think that when he asks me I'll say "Vibrant" but the man he asks, Albero from Abelgorri (?) (xii) doesn't answer.

DREAM 10 Friday 28th Sept.'01 Chinebro

DREAM 10a: In a big tourist attraction – like the World Trade Centre – but in Australia – it could be the Opera House (i). I have seven tourists (ii) with me, adolescents who I want to come up to the top – there's escalators and I think a revolving restaurant (iii) – but one says (a boy) that as it's a holiday w/e there will be so many people so it's best not. Coming down the moving staircases I shout to them to get my bag and laugh about that with a girl beside me. It's Ff. (iv) and we step off the staircase into a roomful of actors rehearsing a play (v). We start dancing to the music (vi) and they're not too happy about that. Outside Ff. asks a woman at reception (vii) if she can join the troupe and afterwards complains that the woman is so English, hesitating and stuttering before saying "yes" and so meaning "no" (viii). Someone is telling me about the layout of a formal garden (ix) planned by Sir Arthur_____ (x). It's very interesting now that I know more. They continue to lay it out in that way even though it's uncomfortable, an L-shaped (xi) bit of white substance like wax or sugar that won't fit in (xii). I meet Mum and I get upset when she tells me about Uncle _____ dying, even though I knew and it was last month (xiii). I've got a book on Forest Gardening (?) (xiv) for him. Back home and I wonder if [my girlfriend] (xv) has turned up yet, I race up to my room and find a pink jumper in process of being knitted (xvi) and a knapsack and a book in Spanish – she's here! (xvii)

DREAM 10b: Bush, Chief of Staff & some other guy are together and they're presenting him with things (i). He's just lain down on his grandmother's grave with something long and blue like a scarf or a Tibetan Prayer Flag then he got up and made a grimace as if "Eh! That's it over" and flipped his hand at the grave in a gesture of dismissal (ii). They present him saying, "There's the Physicalist (iii) (a book) and the Dedication to Harry Potter (iv). He thanks them. Me and my friends are watching the window from a trench, one by one young, unarmed men – some more cautious than others – come out and sit down or stand on the window sill/balcony (v). I think it's a trick but I don't understand why (vi). Meanwhile three young girls – beautiful like the Three Graces – are standing outside of our house and strange lights – atomic energy (vii) particles sent to destroy – come towards them and the house. After the party (viii) I look for the bikes and hey presto! (ix) they've got lights on in the park (x). I'm waiting inside and a little stout man (xi) says that he's German (he means nationalised, I'm sure he's S. American) and that if anyone wants anything to drink, he'll buy them it. Some kids look interested. I'm on the bus then on the pavement and a group of young bearded men in light blue turbans passes me, marching in formation. I think it's the Nation of Islam (xii) and wonder if they'll do anything because I'm white. Indeed three at the end extend their arms (xiii) as if they're going to punch me but they don't. I get into the hotel where I work and an Islamic Canadian guy is washing the dishes (xiv). We talk about the whole situation which must be difficult for him when they confuse him with fundamentalists. I say it's like confusing me with some twit in a tent in the park (xv) shouting and deceiving everyone.

DREAM 11 Saturday 29th September '01, Chinebro [underlined is Spanish]

Saying goodbye to Gf.. (i) Before, I was in a big church singing with the armorial bearing of the Duke of York (iv) like a trident (v) and a little flag like you see in the jousts like "A Knight's Tale" (vi). The important people pass by – a bishop (vii) or whatever and I see that I have the guitar in my hands (viii) and it's someone's (viii). I say to a corpulent Italian man that he sings well (ix) and he likes it but is wary of me. I enter a shop and a pretty girl attends me I explain that the guitar is one of the Duke of York's men (x). We all laugh at that. I say goodbye to Gf. who is working there (xi) – she is in the garden and we talk with a friend of hers, Italian. Jm.? (xii) Xavier (xiii) from Erkametza? who will come with her to visit me. (xiv) He knows a very cheap hotel very nearby with good food and air conditioning. I say that I'll go there too. (xv) In the showers looking for someone. I see the nude body of a guy. (xvi) I see a large parchment like a heraldic charter which is a paper (xvii) that Em. wrote for a conference in Japan about a book about the collapse of the Soviets and Breshnev. It looks very erudite but doesn't make any sense. (xvii) I give up and look at the installation (xx) he's put up beside it – a plot of land with tiny little piles of stones like a Zen garden (xxi). That doesn't make sense either. I go round the back opening cupboards but there's nothing in them (there's a double row of cupboards, (xxii) I open the back row) the last one is marked "extinguisher". (xxiii)

DREAM 12 Sunday 30th Sept. '01 Chinebro

In a lift – a whole room like the back storeroom of a kitchen or a toolshed – I press the upper of two metal buttons (i) and go up, shaking (ii). The wall opens and I see the stairs and duck out through a door passing the right door on the right and get out the back where there's a path (iii) full of men working (iv). An old wizened brown man has bloated muscles on his arms and I think he's worked physically hard all his life (v). I go up a path and remember there's a way out of Jordanhill Training College (vi). A fly gets in my left ear and I flush it out – it's dead (vii). Someone was with me in the lift – I think it was Dm. (viii) – he had to get home (ix). Before that there was a room full of people. The room is bottle-shaped, like a womb. (x)

DREAM 13 Monday 1st October '01 Chinebro

DREAM 13a: In the forest with the guys from Ilargialdi. I'm wondering where they can all sleep (i). A girl says it's her birthday (ii) and that five of her students proposed (iii). There's a dancing class in St. Flannans Church, I'm in a room at the back with people (iv) and I say that whoever it was took my tape? it must be someone in the advanced class because you can hear it on the tape, the rhythm (v). There are very few people in the class.

DREAM 13b I arrive latest at the combat class. We have to drop off a smooth curved wall from various heights (i). A guy has done the highest – I'm glad as I'm afraid. The instructress (ii) is talking so I just slip in as you do when late for a lecture. After class I go and talk to her, we'd had to throw a metal pole with a square bolted to it ("like a javelin" she said) and she says " I see you've done Ju-Jitsu (or Aikidu) (iii) and I say I've done Capoeira and T'ai Chi. Later I introduce a guy to some fierce motorbiking females and off they go on something between Harley Davidsons (iv) and a scary ride in capsules spinning about at the Fairground (v). They have a problem and I climb up from a garden wall to help them escape from the wreckage (vi).

DREAM 13c Having to play basketball with the others and feeling that I'll never be any good at it.(i)

DREAM 13d Snogging Km.. (i)

DREAM 14 Tuesday 2nd Oct. '01 Chinebro

I'm looking at the river of the Pilgrim's Way to Santiago – at one point it goes underground for a short distance as the waterpipe does in Chinebro. I think that I would try and get in from there, not from further up because I wouldn't be able to survive such a lot of time underground (i). I think that H-B3f. wouldn't be able to do the next part as she would get stuck she's too big and someone would have to explain diplomatically (ii). Then I realise I'd have claustrophobia as it's underground and goes round a bend (iii). They've diverted the river into the monastery (iv) and will transplant a lot of flowers next year – that's good as there are lots of thorns this year, thorny bushes (v). I go into the monastery and meet Br. Nick (vi) who's got loads of books and stuff – it's heavy. The other postulant is with him. I divide the stuff in three and arrange that we'll all go different ways (vii) to try and find Fr. Cassian (viii) and then meet up back there and put the stuff where he wants to put it – I suggest the St. Bernard/ Benedict? Iona? (ix) room. I go upstairs and end up in the library (x) and see him after I see Fr. Agnellus (xi) – he's wearing white (xii) and recognises me even though it's been fifteen years I say, "Yes, I'm a postulant again" and ask him about the books. He says that they usually (the kitchen staff) won't let him into the Thistle Chamber (Centre?/ Room?) (xiii) but to try. If not I say about the other place. I meet someone and tell them I forgot Cassian's name and say, "Tall, white hair with a slight scar on his chin" (xiv), "Mart" (Mark?) they say (xv).

DREAM 15 Wednesday 3rd Oct. '01 Chinebro

Cars everywhere (i) all over the road, a mother gets out of a car and picks something up – a food – and I ask "What's McBruck?" They are surprised and pleased at the question and say it means "Yuck" (iii) . I ask why they are preparing it – is there a party tonight but quickly add that I'm not hinting for an invitation – I'm going to see a play. The play was supposed to start at 6.30 but I left

70

to go there at 6.30 but being actors they'll be late (iv). I get to the play – some girl gives me a sweet and I give it to the actors. I go up the back and am going to sit beside a girl that I think I recognise (vi) but when I put my glasses on it isn't her. I sit anywhere and a young English guy beside me says "Hello" – he's reading the newspaper – then we have a conversation. (vii)

DREAM 16a Thursday 4th October '01, Chinebro

DREAM 16a: I lower myself down to the level of the tunnel and I see If. sitting there, ready to sell football entrances. I say that my friend wanted to know if the kitchen (i) was open as he got no answer from them. Her father (ii) is here, in Scotland, and she will go North and visit him but not tomorrow, "Tomorrow I'll stay in my room" (iii) she says. She's got a bit of a cold (iv) (she has water on her shoulders) and I know two friends will be disappointed as they really wanted to go tomorrow (v).

DREAM 16b In a big banqueting hall at Christmas. I go out to the corridor and a girl is there, stealing the Christmas cake and laughing (i) – it belongs to a rich man and is made of plums (ii). I help her and run down the corridor, turning left. I think she should go downstairs to the right and eat it on the little landing above the entrance hall but she disappears. I go further on – into the chapel. The choir are practising there and I ask for B2m. (iii). He's not there, he got thrown out by the guy in charge for messing about with the chorus (iv). I think that I'll have to see him alone – without his wife as she's always around when we're together (v). The church is like All Saints in St. Andrews (vi).

DREAM 17 Friday 5th Oct. '01 Chinebro

Two women talking – one has to do an operation on the other and is making excuses saying that she'll put the woman on "general?" meaning that any doctor in the clinic might do it – including her. (i) Going past a *Guardería* (ii) [nursery] a woman posts her baby through a little box (iii) and her little son walks under a bar (iv) to go inside too. Mum is inside looking for a woman – to make sure it's alright. My sister B1f. says to me that mum has a way of finding people and still be alright. (vi) Upstairs in another building – a sports club – I find a little cat with a name tag "Macnab" I wonder if it's Heather's. (vii) I ask a friend's opinion and find the name "Guidance F.H." and we both laugh – it's got to be Heather's, it's such a strange name. (viii) A middle-aged woman comes out and asks me when Mercedes **[71]** (one of my students) comes to the club – no point coming alone when you can come together she says. I'm surprised that she comes at all at her age. (ix) I help lift her trolley down some stairs and she almost falls but is ok and unruffled. (x) Going down in the loft a big lad who's got mental health problems (xi) opens the lift door to get a police cone (xii) on the other side. I'm sitting in front of three black guys who are talking about what "good shit" their drugs were (xiii) and I jump over to take the lad's hand and lead him towards the door – now open. We don't even know where or when he's supposed to meet Heather. I hope I'm doing the right thing. (xiii)

NOTES

[71] Like 'Heather', unidentifiable, Spanish Marian name meaning "mercy".

DREAM 18 Saturday 6th Oct. '01 Chinebro

A bar in the middle of the desert (i). The barman/D.J. is doing the usual happy hours (ii) and commentaries. A gorgeous woman, made up and accessorised and very girlie, runs off suddenly for a date with a man (iii). The whole bar cheers and laughs. The D.J. announces, "5p (iv) drinks at the bar if you got it" (meaning this week)(v). I order a drink as does a girl beside me (vi). I imagine that if they ask me I'll say "Pedro, his name is Pedro."(vii).

DREAM 20 Monday 8th Oct '01 Chinebro

A family of Germans (i) comes to live in Erkametza and meet me. I'm really surprised because they're clean (ii). There's the parents and a young girl of marriageable age and a little girl (iii) at least I think so because they've all got so much hair – like the Hill Billy Bunch in Penelope Pitstop and the Whacky Races (iv). I show them around and am worried in case they get fleas (v). The little girl is very sweet but by mistake her knapsack is left out in the rain (vi). She asks if there are any kids to play with, "there are in Finko" I say. "Finko" she repeats with disdain (vii). The older girl is going to get married and we have to plan a complicated trajectory for her to reach her destination. The map could either be from Erkametza to somewhere down on the left to down on the right (vii) or from Germany to Spain to Italy (ix). She could go straight of course – I don't see why she doesn't (x). The map is heavily wooded (xi). I walk into a room and it's full of my school/ university friends, but older (xii). I recognise so many people and we're very happy to see each other: B3m. from Primary School – C2f. from Uni who introduces me to her lover! Female, who's Spanish. I find out she's her lover when I translate for them *"amante"*. I first translate "lover" then as "friend" but C2f. corrects me (xiii). Afterwards I have to wait (to eat?) until twenty past eight (xiv). I think Dave from Uni is there (xv). I'm with my sister B1f. and her boyfriend (xvi) in a *"furgonetta"* (camper van) (xvii) and he's talking about her bust (xviii), I tell him to calm down and tell them we're driving along between the wall and another *"furgo"* which we can't get past as the door is open – I talk to them and they shut the door and drive off. Just as well because an angry gang leader is just behind us (xix). I have to run to catch up with [brother-in-law] and when I do it's a street full of people listening to an Indian Maharishi guru. He smiles at me – I'd put my hands together and bowed at him and I know he's going to call me to him. (xx). He says "and now we're going to have Scottish dancing (xxi) and I and a girl get up. The there's another girl but we're trying to do the Gay Gordons and it's difficult, they don't really know it and the music is too slow (xxii). I want the girls to merge together but they don't so eventually I get in the middle, take both their hands and make up the dance (xxiii).

DREAM 21 Tuesday 9th October '01 Erkametza

DREAM 21a: Female visitors are coming to the *pueblo* (i) (village). The place is a mess – all sticks and mud. I go around trying to put the sticks together (ii) but I don't know if I'm doing it for their benefit (and if all the *pueblo* is behind me) (iii) or if I'm going to *sequestrárles* (iv) (kidnap them).

DREAM 21(b) On a ship. I shove my stuff in my room but I've got no time to sort it out (i).[I have censored this part](ii). She goes upstairs (iii) and says "hold on guys" as we continue – he's also someone else (iv). I go to see if there's a free breakfast, there's a long baguette with some cheese on it and coffee (v). I go to tell everyone but my sister B1f. is organising things with other women in the kitchen – one's got her head up the chimney so I leave them (vi). A group of mean little boys is on board – I hope they won't be tiresome (viii). I meet guys with back-packs whom I used to fancy (like Fm. from the Hostel) and say "just keep your back-pack on and keep walking, right over the rails" (viii) I go to get breakfast but passing a bar the *moreno* [brown] guy chucks something at me – his aim is great it nearly hits me and goes spinning about in the air to everyone's admiration (ix). I look down and see people eating on the benches. If I'm late and it's closed I'm going to say that my family are there (x). I get back to my room – it's a mess but my blue clasp of my keyring is there with my key (xi).

DREAM 22 Wednesday 10th Oct. '01 Erkametza

DREAM 22a: Talking with a girl in a bar and hearing the news report in my head of how she killed herself at the same time (i). At first I'm upstairs and I'm going to meet Ff. for a teachers' get-together / training course (ii). We're going to watch something on t.v. I could have watched it on the wide screen in the bar (iii) though and when I go downstairs to the toilet, she comes in with loads of little jars (iv) (face creams and a mirror it seems) in her hand but I can hear in my head (v) that she killed herself slowly like what they did to Wallace (vi). She was waiting for her boyfriend (vii). I wanted a sandwich at the bar but he really didn't have anything. I could have done something. (viii).

DREAM 22b: Outside some building on the corner (i). Pairs of spies are following everyone (ii). A man and a woman are nodded at to follow me. I go to an office newspaper office? (iii) and talk with a really nice guy, B1m.? Lm.? (iv) The spies are in the next room and I tell him about them – I look in they are in a state of undress and sulky. I march them out and he tells me off. (v)

DREAM 22c: In a corridor, beside lockers with Df. (i) – it's the end of the academic day (ii) we're putting stuff away and chatting.

DREAM 23 Thursday 11th Oct. '01 Erkametza

"The Mounties always get their man."

DREAM 24 Friday 12th Oct. '01 Erkametza

There's a competition for women in bathing suits to leap from ice-floe to ice-floe and finally to do a long jump and slide along the floor artistically.(i) I think my wife will win.(ii) In the swimming-pool the boys are doing a demonstration but they are too long under the water.(iii) I can see the yellow of their tee-shirts.(iv) I take a deep breath and dive down, I find a weight in the water and go deeper, flailing my arms to find people – I find one boy (v) and push him up to the surface – the tee-shirt is red now. (vi) Then another (vii). But when I get back up there are still some missing. I dive again and find one and we put him in a tent and give him oxygen too and take some myself (ix). Back at the surface, they want me to investigate but the boss doesn't have much confidence in me (x). I tell the girl that I want the pool illuminated (xi) (there's a Boy Scout group in a small section of it now learning to swim with an instructress) (xii) and the boss isn't very convinced but he says

"Yes" (xiii). As we talk about this we walk through a park with lots of animals covered with volcanic ash – they are waking up and shaking it off (xiv). I call some to me and pat them – one is made up of tin plates and is completely mythical (it's based on a post box) (xv) I tell the girl. Another big like one tries to bite me and think it's better not to let it get my arm but my torso as it could bite my arm off – it's a problem that needs solving (xvi) I get to the swimming pool and see a duck and a nest floating about and wonder how they got in (xvii). On the other side there's, not catamarans (xviii) but kayaks and canoes and little boats. I go to the next room and see the same – I'll take one out. I also see a pile of small rugs tapestries of shawls and some articles by Idries Shah (xix) In the middle I find silken Spanish money, then lots of folded peseta paper money (xx). It must belong to someone so I'll leave it here I put it all back as I hear footsteps. It's Ricardo – he wants to tell me something and I don't really listen (xxi). I tell him that we must go to London on Friday and go out in the little boats and discover the truth (xxii).

DREAM 25 Saturday 13th Oct. '01 Erkametza

On a lawn between University buildings – like Magdalen College (i) or St. Andrews (ii) – a woman shows me a grave underneath a building, it has a railing and gravel and looks Victorian (iii). The name is "Abigail" (iv) and above, on the headstone, is an engraving of Thoth, the Egyptian vulture god, taking her soul to heaven (v). I explain this to the woman (vi). She says that there's a serial on t.v. where Brad Pitt is trapped in the body of a schoolboy (vii), there's a scene – which is spread over many pages – where he kisses a girl and the girl writes how she feels (viii). The woman has cut these pages out for me and tells me she'll put them in an envelope and give me them when I go (ix). "Shit!" she says, "I've got a husband and children" (x). She pushes away, playfully but purposefully, a couple of guys who are so closely arm-in-arm they look like Siamese twins (xi). They turn round and I'm surprised to see that they're Western (xi). I think that the woman is so much in control – she organised this whole University event (open day or something) – and yet she's not of her heart because she's in love with me and I'm not with her (xiii). I feel sorry for her. (xiv)

DREAM 26 Sunday 14th Oct. Erkametza

Someone gives me strips of paper or material (i). I have a box/compartment made of red plastic (ii) which, because it's joined onto others you can't see the nametag that I put on (iii). I get another one and stop the first years (iv) using it. I give them laundry powder and explain about the machines – they're going to wash some of my stuff with theirs (v). I'm in the bus station and I think that you really miss people but it's nice when they go too (vi). Reading a book from Jf. to Harry the dedication is confused. (vii)

DREAM 27 Monday 15th Oct. Erkametza

Northern Ireland: "With their tanks and their guns, oh my God what have they done, to the town I loved so well" (i) I'm in a church (ii). Kf. (iii) and a group of women come in and start haranguing the priest for saying an altar mass (iv) and demanding to know why, I had supported them before but I didn't feel like it now so I leave discreetly (v). I have to go to or make a meal (vi).

DREAM 28 Tuesday 16th Oct. Erkametza

I could sleep in the house at the back but it's not very welcoming – there's nothing there (i). I go to get four story tapes (Harry Potter) (ii) and I see Lf./m.(iii) sitting at a table wearing a white hawk mask (iv) like in Carnival in Venice (v). Mine is better (vii). I say I'm leaving for a trip shortly – to Africa I think (viii) – we have a civilised chat and then I go away (ix).

DREAM 29 Wednesday 17th Oct. Erkametza

Mum bought a house off an old woman – who I think went into a home (i). I go there and it's really dark and I don't know why Mum bought it – but then I open the curtains and it's better (ii). The children – two young guys and a girl – are at first a bit aggressive to me (iii). I boil water and they take it but then I do something stupid with the chips? (iv) and we all laugh and they help me to put it under the grill (v). In another place and Carla comes out of the cupboard wearing a lavender shawl and with her hair space–age and purple (vi). A guy come out after in a lavender blouse (vii). I'm eating a light bulb shaped like a lollypop and they wonder at that (viii). Some guys – I think *Ettaras* – come to the village and I welcome them and show them around. (ix)

DREAM 30 Thurs. 18th Oct '01 Erkametza

Talking to the three female bosses of the English School – by telephone (i). I say that this time I'm not going to work so hard and burn myself out (ii). Walking back up a street and I think I should buy something as I won't be able to once I get back to the community (iii). I try to think what we need/ want. A big Black guy comes up to me and puts one arm around me.(iv) I smile and try not to instantly presume just because he's Black he's going to mug me. (v) Then he gets out his flick knife. I think where my wallet is. Someone's speaking with me with admiration of the community as if it's a monastic order. Such simple life (vi). I say there's no need to go to the Basque Country for that – there's the Carmelites down the road. (vii)

DREAM 31 Fri. 19th Oct '01 Erkametza [Underlined is Spanish]

Carla lets something fall (i) and I pick it up, it's something ceramic and alien. The Finn[ish guy] says "Yes, we're aliens and I'll show you."["you" is plural, familiar]. I'm trying to cross the road up at Spar (iv) and I do with a woman who's talking with her daughter, blue (v). I don't know which bus to take to St. Agatha's/ Oxgang school, whichever I say the bus driver will know whether I'm Catholic or Protestant (vi). I walk to the corner – a little minibus goes the wrong way (along the top road) I walk down the hill a little. I must learn where the buses go and when (vii).

DREAM 32 Sat. 20th Oct '01 Erkametza

With Dave from the village – Ricardo and someone are inside. We have to get them out and leave in search of food and shelter (i). The three nuns we can't take with us but they're nuns – they'll survive (ii). I go out and find bulls penned in and a notice on the gate (iii). Their food is outside and I shout at them to go back while I put it in – opening the gate (iv). Maybe we could make a sled or something (v). I'm brushing my teeth (vi) and my aunt Mf. is criticising me – she's with my Mum who's laughing – I say "Why do you always have to be so critical?" She'll probably only deny it but it's true (vii). A great *chorro* (torrent/ stream) of water runs off the hut /church – it's the neighbour he's watering the garden or something and doesn't realise (viii).

Appendix B: Ethnopoetry

As noted for Dream 2, the condensation and over-determination operating in the dreams problematise their easy classification into groups, as does the mix of previous and present relationships and ethnographic information. Freud (1988) found many similarities between poetry and dream – it was this which enabled me to analyse the poetry of san Juan de la Cruz – and so I have used the ethnopoems written about the two communities as an organising principle. As each of the stanzas is either dedicated to one member of the community (in "Erkamertza") or a subject (in "Chinebro"), I can thus introduce L.C. dream material [72] and also adhere to Cohen's above quoted rule that the ethnographer should "regard social groups as a collection of complex selves".

NOTES

[72] While referring to the M.C. appended, below, under Dreams.

1: Erkamertza

Un@ Anarkist@ Perfekt@ A Perfect Anarchist
¿kién pueda hallarl@? who can find her?
Se levanta kon el sol a poner la levadura madre, a encender el fuego:
She rises with the sun to start the mother-yeast, to start the fire:
hace txapatis, korte pan pone el ajo, aceite, la sal pone tomate,
she makes chapatis, cuts bread, sets out garlic, oil, salt,
la mermelada (ambos hetxos en kasa) todo biológico – todo integral.
the tomatoes, marmalade (both homemade, both organic),
A l'agua hirviendo etxa hierba Luisa, tomillo, inojo, toka la kontxa: esperar.
to boiling water she adds lemongrass, thyme, dill, sounds the conch; waiting.

3(vii) A1f., like me, is Virgo and could symbolise practicality as she's extremely well-organised. 3(viii)… Maybe after working the previous day with Carla in the kitchen I feel more integrated into the community. After a meal in the flat of one of the cooks of the restaurant I commented to Gf. that we had made up a spontaneous and transitory community and that it felt nice – like here.

6c(iv) …the "older woman" must be a mother figure – perhaps my own and also one/both of the Spanish girls in the village who are most central to the community.

9(v) …a couple of days previously, Carla (talking about shoplifting) used the word "*morbo*" (thrill) which reminded me of Im. talking of his boyfriend and calling him "*morboso*" (thrill-seeking/ horny) when talking of their open relationship.

21b(v) Breakfast was quite an ordeal in Chinebro, here I'm looking forward to a big Erkametza breakfast of toast and marmalade / herbal tea, porridge and fruit. 21b(x) Declaration of kinship as the key to entrance to the communal kitchen. Maybe I'm worried that I've slept too long or that I've been away too long and the confidence I'd built up has evaporated.

22a(iv) Carla from Erkametza, when I and Miguel and she went "recycling" in Iruñea was given a lot of little tubes of natural cosmetic/ medicinal things by a Co-op. She decided to use some for herself.

Vienen de kasas arruinadas They come from ruined houses
donde han repuesto las vigas, tejado, tetxo, ventanas, puerta kon
bisagra
where they've replaced the beams, ceiling, roofs, windows, doors
with hinges
y sin cerradura: son tod@s Anarkist@s no les hace falta.
and without locks: they're anarchists, they don't need them.
Vienen de tiendas viejas de campaña o del boske de pasar la
notxe en estrella.
They come from tents or from the wood from starry vigil,
Vienen kon sus sueños aún vivos – kon ropa rasgada y kosida kon
flores.
they come with their dreams still alive, with torn clothing sewn
with flowers.

2c(vii) The "yard" could be an exercise yard in a prison camp –
indeed "*Frontón*" is a Basque sport and that yard [of the *Gaztetxe*] in
Pamplona was the scene of massive police / anarchist conflict when
the former came to throw the latter out who took refuge in the
scaffolding in a box and then threw stuff at the police – as did the
neighbours. 2c(viii) "*Gaztetxe*" is Basque for "house of youth" and
nearby in Pamplona is the Refuge for the Pilgrims to Santiago…
21a(ii) In fact Erkametza is well organised and tidy – as *okupa*
villages go – coming back from Chinebro I was quite disgruntled as
full of cold with my voice gone.
24(xiv) Jurrasic park? The Land that Time Forgot? Someone said
that the Finnish girl (who wears reindeer fur and hippy skirts and
braided hair) looks like a character from a film of primitive people.
31(iii) "*El Finlandés*" means a male Finnish person, in fact his
female friend had gone to a meditation course in Barcelona. The
previous night I was looking at him – he's very boyish and pretty –
and thinking how alien he is. He was singing in Finnish as well and I
remarked to Rebecca that it's not even Indo-European. Maybe as he
(and she) are so alien it makes me feel more akin to the community.

Se besan. They kiss,
Besan en la boca – a la Rusa – hombres y mujeres
kiss on the mouth – like Russians – men and women
igual de kariño igual de kamarad. Fuman, hablan, beben,
equally tender, equally comrades. They smoke, speak, drink,
komen y konkordan en la tarea del día:
eat and agree on the tasks of the day:
hay la huerta, la kasa, limpiar ropas, kocinar.
there's the kitchen garden, the house, clothes to wash, cooking.

7b(ii) Working in the Youth Hostel I thought a lot about kinship and trust among travellers and commented on it to [my supervisor].

9(x) When Hm. met an old friend from Brazil, in Edinburgh, I was struck by them kissing on the cheeks. Here in the villages, everyone, male and female has adopted the habit (which I believe to be originally Russian) of kissing everyone on the mouth. Even so there is a slight variation depending on intimacy – normally upon meeting people for the first time, if one of you is not confident of being really in, you would shake hands or kiss on the cheeks instead. 9(xii) Albero is older and quite dignified, the previous day I banged into his nose when I kissed him but he took it in his stride. He puts forward his opinions at length.

22a(ii) The previous night Xavier mentioned a week-long training course in consensus to be held in one of the villages.

24(xiv)…Ash we use from the stove (like an Aga) for the *Kakaleku* (Basque for "shit-place") to wash our hands as it has a detergent and sterilising action.

26(v) …Here we use soap made of pigs' grease, salt and ash which dissolves naturally with grease. I sometimes add a little laundry to other people's if it's lying in soak. Usually we leave it soaking for 24 hours then use the washboard and rinse and hang it up to dry.

28(vii) This was always a sore point: Lf. in drag always wanted kissed as a woman and not shaken by the hand as a man – I always found it embarrassing but didn't want to show anti-transvestite feelings or lack of gay solidarity. There may be a reference in the dream to pantomime or to Judas' kiss as there is some confusion of partners [in the community] and subsequent jealousy. 28(viii) A desire to have a break and go far away. Is the "dark continent" my subconscious? 32(vi) The community makes a big thing of this and the interminable toothbrushing in the kitchen drives me mad – especially as the people tend to walk about doing things in the process.

Uno hace una mesa, One is making a table,
al pino blanko una kapa de aceite: a los pies, linaza, a la tabla,
oliva.
on the blond pine a coat of oil: on the legs linseed, on the tabletop
olive.
Trabaja lento y bién, no habla, kanta – le mira un petirrojo.
He works slowly and well, singing – a robin watches.
El sol koje el juego de sus musklos ke ya han hetxo una kama,
The sun catches the play of his muscles that have already built a
bed,
larga y firme, sencilla komo la vida.
large and firm, simple as Life.

COMMENT 7a(i) At first I thought that I wouldn't get on with
Dave in the village but then I discovered that I really liked him
ANALYSIS 7a(iv) Dave of the village is red haired and attractive
and yesterday we were talking about the fluidity of sexual attraction.

20(xxi) …Dave in Erkametza has been to India and acquired the
habits that western hippies do. 20(xix) Dave from the village has a
bodhran case saying 'London please'.

27(iv) Often groups of radical Catholics – especially women –
question the need for a priest. One solution is to have an "*agape*"
and not a mass. The theological problem is whether the priesthood
which is charismatically in the people and the priesthood which is
sacramentally in the priest – has the same authority. Perhaps this was
prompted by the absence of Dave from the previous evening's
tertullia (chat over wine or food). With him it would have been an
asamblea, an anarchist assembly to decide about action in the
village. There hasn't been one for about five weeks and many jobs in
the village are held up for lack of direction. I have been saying that
we need a temporary, working, plan. 27(v) During the *tertuallia* – I
gave up trying to get Dave to attend it – I was either in the kitchen or
the house as I couldn't be bothered to listen in but got bits of it from
people who went in and out (it was round a campfire, where we eat,
outside the church) and felt that on the whole it was good that some
issues were being cleared up and voiced before the official
asamblea. 27(vi) I'm sure this is breakfast but the question is to join
in (as an equal) or to make it (to preside). In R.C. theology the priest
is the president of the sacred meal – the liturgy – and when one

priest moved his chair in front of the altar to emphasis this (in our parish at home) my father compared it to the replacement in fascist Italy of the crucifix by a poster of Mussolini. Maybe I'm facing questions of participation in decisions and afraid of exercising too much authority and trying to take responsibility for how that may be see. This problem is not new for ethnographers: see [73].

28(i) A couple has formed in the back room of the house (I sleep in the connecting front room) they woke us all up the previous morning. Because of this, and because of feeling for one of them, Dave moved to a tent. I was annoyed at so many people in the house …The morning of the dream it took me a while to remember my dream as so many people were stomping about.

31(iii) The previous day Dave asked me to come to future meetings to facilitate and help with language comprehension – it made me feel part of it and aware of how good my Spanish and grasp of slang is.

NOTES

[73] Writing the ANALYSIS in the community I'd forgotten the reference. It is: "In the field I developed some principles that I would now call uninvolved paternalism. I now see my responsibility to the people I study to be to deal with the problems that concern them as well as with those that interest me." (Rynkiewich & James/1976/59)

Alta, (pañuelo azul sobre la kabeza) Tall, (blue kerchief on her
head),
una corta mimbre; las tijeras de podar debajo de una yema,
one cuts willow; the secateurs below a bud,
kada eskeje medida justa – komo la Ley no es.
each cutting measured justly – as the Law is not.
Rekoje a la vez los mimbres y sus pensamientos:
She recollects at the same time the willows and her thoughts:
de las kabras los guarda una cerka ke hizo ayer;
a fence she made yesterday will guard them from the goats;
¿kién la guarda de la Guardia Civil?
who will guard her from the Civil Guard?

7a(ix) Rebecca in the village wanted to have a ceilidh when I said
I knew ceilidh dances.

9(viii) Rebecca was to come too ["to Chinebro"] but at the last
minute got an official letter which she thought was about a court
appearance… 9(ix) Rebecca eventually turned up, her robotic
movements in the dream remind me of Coppelia and of Spanish
performers in Covent Garden, London. I felt that she wasn't free
when she instantly changed her plans because of the letter.

20(xvii) …could also represent any of the girls here with whom I
have a fraternal relationship.

22a(i) The previous night (I passed the entire day in silence to
heal my throat) I'd overheard Rebecca and Dave speaking. She
seemed sad. I feel fraternally towards her but I feel she feels more –
a desire to comfort her and guilt that I should be more affectionate
(which of course could also be concealed desire and the guilt due to
the fraternal relationship which we have). 22a(vi) "Braveheart" is the
obvious adjective. Rebecca quite inspires me – she reminds me of La
Passionara the famous Italian anarchist whose statue is by the banks
of the Clyde. 22a(viii) The juxtaposition of these two needs shows
me that I'm being selfish: that in fact I'm okay but some people are
not and I could help them.22b(ii) "Spies" a constant preoccupation
with how the community views my work, and also a sense of
eavesdropping as I couldn't help overhearing the conversation
between Dave and Rebecca the previous night. 22b(iii) Newspaper
offices remind me of Clark Kent – Superman. 22b(iv) B1m. is a
lawyer and Lm. an air steward. B1m. is extremely attractive and

athletic and Lm. flies – superman in his office? 22b(v) "A nice guy" a "super man" Lois Lane's words, doesn't eavesdrop? Superman as Übermann as superego / conscience?

31(v) I wonder if this woman and her daughter who kept appearing is Rebecca and her mother. The previous night I complimented her on her breadmaking skill (everyone else's turns out flat) and said that her mother was right (she wanted her to open a Bakery) and that the world had gained a perfect anarchist (the title of a poem I wrote for them the other day which they're going to publish in an anarchist/ *okupa* magazine, the verses changed from the Bible – Proverbs "A Perfect Wife") and lost a great baker (or baxter to be exact and Mary Dalyish!)

Mono azul Blue overalls
y kabeza ke rekuerda la fuerza maskulina de los Moros;
and a head reminiscent of the manly strength of the Moors;
él está konstuyendo un arko de medio punto sobre una ventanilla.
he is constructing a half-pointed arch over a little window.
Son once los ladrillos y las personas en el pueblo:
Eleven are the bricks and the people in the village:
su hacer – komo el cimento – les pone en harmonía.
he handles them and cements them together in harmony.

8(i) When I visited Gf. and Mm. … in Edinburgh, we met up with a network of Spanish people in the Scottish capital. Pepe, newly arrived the previous day in Erkametza, used the same word, "red " in Spanish, to refer to the inter–related communities of foreigners (mostly English and German) in S.E. Spain who practise permaculture. I had lived for a summer in one such community, Orgiva, in the Sierra Nevada where Gerald Brennan lived and wrote his famous book "South from Granada" and Pepe had worked in another community of Germans who study greening the desert by specialised seeds. Thus I was able to draw him and Pamela (who's German) and Dave into the conversation. I was pleased that my "networking" helped such disparate people to bond.

29(vi) Lavender/ coming out of the closet – gay/ lesbian connotations. Carla may be bisexual but I don't know. 29(vii) Big girl's blouse? I don't connect this with any events of the previous day. I felt at first that Pepe was attracted to Carla and maybe in the dream he's "after her" (the same expression in Spanish) and as I find him attractive I wish that he's gay (and that she's lesbian). If she was it would cut out the competition – Rebecca. I feel there's more to it than this.

Primero de trabajar First to work
último de akabar; donde la eskalera hace la eskina, kon paciencia
y dedicación,
last to stop, at the turn of the stairs, with patience and dedication,
está poniendo eskalones, kon madera de antes de la reforestación.
he is putting up steps with wood from before the reforestation.
Aprende Euskera, eskalón por eskalón, palabra por palabra:
He's learning Basque, step by step, word by word:
Gora Erkametza! Gora Okupak!
¡Gora Erkametza! ¡Gora Okupak! **[74]**

4(i) The immediate reference is to the fact that the bridge is so long, when they stop painting at one end it's time to start at the other – so something interminable. The previous day we cleared rubble from outside the "house" and it felt like this.

4(ii) There could be phallic allusions to "long" and "up" especially as (Ricardo having company in the tent) the previous night I slept in the house in the same bed as Xavier. Also it could refer to keeping up with the others in terms of the work which supports the structure. The previous day we unearthed a column which had been used to support another room of the house (now crumbled) and I joked with Xavier about it being a girl ("Pilar " is Spanish for "pillar" and is a common, Marian, name). 4(iv) "No man is an island" Xavier seems to be so but quietly supports the community with his continual work. I feel I have managed to reach out and touch him.

NOTES

[74] Basque: *Gora* is 'up'/ 'viva'. *Okupak* is the plural form of the loan word from Spanish: *okupa*.

Kozinando la komida Cooking lunch
(después de fregar todos los platos del día anterior)
(after washing all the dishes from the day before),
eskutxa y kanta kon Radio Euskadi mientras asa patatas,
he listens to Radio Euskadi while he bakes potatoes,
remueve un guiso de verduras de la huerta y kon kuatro estígmas
stirs a stew of vegetables from the garden and with four stamens
del flor del azafrán hace del arroz, oro y del aire, sabor.
of saffron–flowers he makes of the rice, gold and of the air,
savour.

6a(i) Perhaps a reference to the Tarot/cards in dream one –
Master/Jack of Trades. The previous day I made scones which were
deemed a great success by the community and I felt good especially
as I'd passed the morning in a bad mood after the difficult climb of
the night before.

20(xix) A shadow figure? ETA? with whom our relation is one of
tacit approval but not direct connection (which would complicate our
position politically) with many people in the villages condemning
violence – but not all.

21a(iv) This screams ETA, the Basque separatist group who often
kidnap people for ransom. There's an obvious sexual power play but
also we increasingly joke about being terrorists as the police use
anti–terrorist laws to detain *okupa*s (although the judges usually
throw the cases out of court when it finally gets to trial.)

21b(i) …storage space in the villages is limited.

26(iii) Since Joshua came back and I did from Chinebro, I've
been sleeping in the house and I moved all my stuff there. There
have been questions of claiming space for sleeping and possessions.

29(iv) Chips go on fire because of water in the oil: burn water?
Cook badly? The previous day I sorted out the rotten and good fruit
and veg although I left some outside and was slightly criticised for
this. 29(v) Four days previously **[75]** (Saturday) I roasted potatoes in
the oven and was annoyed when the woman I was cooking with kept
opening the oven to check if they were done – thus cooling the oven!

NOTES

[75] Freud usually counts the previous day but my paranoia about the oven door, especially when making scones, was continual and a source of great amusement to the community.

El sol ya konoce The sun is familiar
su kuerpo moreno y el viento su sudor, kava desde la kasa
with his brown body and the wind with his sweat, he is digging
from the house
hasta la pista el desague de tejas; usa el nivel para ver
to the track a tiled drain; he uses the spirit-level to see
ke l'agua bajasse. Baja a la huerta él: regadas, las plantas
that the water runs down. He goes down to the kitchen garden, the
plants
agradecen l'agua komo la gente el perdón.
as grateful for the water as are people for pardon.

2a(iv)…The water source is a natural spring and all water has to
be carried uphill to the kitchen (a roofed Sacristy of a roofless
church) a five minute walk.

10b(iii) Ricardo and I (see Dream One) were discussing who was
who: Materialist and Idealist between the constructors of the
polemical dam and the *okupa* villages. I said the anarchists were
materialists because they were more concerned with appearance than
underlying form so espoused Romanticism and not Classicism [see
Pirsig and Paglia].

11 (xxiii) …the previous day I said to Pancho that his brother
Ricardo is really academic and probably misses studying (he studied
Philisosphy in Granada when I was studying Theology) and it would
be good if he could combine it in some way.

24(xx) The previous night Ricardo and I discussed communal and
private economy and how some people may have personal money at
home or in an account but couldn't use it here or only for long trips
etc. 24(xxi) I'm very voluble and was aware that the previous night
when we went to the crossroads for a walk, I talked the whole time.
24(xxii) I wrote this on a Friday. The next Friday would be the 19th
(no obvious significance). Ricardo and I sometime want to go to
Asturias where the government has granted a seigniorial house to
Pablo and comrades – we may join the community.

31(ii) Ricardo also broke **[76]** a glass bottle on the stairs of the
church last night when he was cooking and went out into the
darkness for something. Almost all kitchen utensils are stored up at
the altar end on a rack – there's no roof on the church. He was
cooking with a big ceramic dish and Rebecca told me that Xavier

had brought one to the village on a roof-rack and that it broke when they got here – and we told Ricardo to be careful as he was jerking it about (as the recipe says).

32(viii) We used to pee off the wall outside the house – until Ricardo installed a plastic cut-off bottle (and I put a lemon in it on a wire). We still do off the wall outside the church. I had shifted sleeping places the previous night so my "neighbour" was an acrobat who was visiting and who I'd seen bathing (quite a common occurrence here) down at the spring. The hosepipe is obviously phallic (I remember being impressed!)

NOTES

[76] The previous notes refers to the fact that Carla "let something fall": 31(i) She did the previous night – a red dress and a toothbrush – but I didn't see what until after I'd written the dream.

Surgiendo de la mar Arising from the sea
de mantas en la kasa, por las ventanas abiertas
of blankets in the house, through open windows
sus ojos vean la belleza ke kiere; sus labios soplan aliento dulce
her eyes behold the beauty that she loves; her lips make sweet
breathy music
en músika, por su flauta. Buskó setas ella por el monte.
through her flute. She sought mushrooms on the mountain
Kon unas kocinará esta notxe, kon otras soñará.
with some she will cook tonight: with others she will dream.

2c(ii) …My father wore his kilt during W.W.II and I was annoyed
the previous night when Richardo mentioned in front of Pamela
(who's German) that my father spent five years in a concentration
camp – actually a farm labour camp.

20(i) "*German*" in Catalan (my girlfriend's language) is "brother"
as in Old English. The word could therefore demonstrate ambivalent
kinship. My father was in a German Labour Camp and so normally
the nationality has a negative value for me but this year especially
I've tried to heal this – with German friends. 28(ix) ... "Africa" was
also the name of a woman with whom my flatmate in [a Spanish
city] was sleeping – despite having a girlfriend and a few other
lovers. This example is very apt here at the moment in the village.

32(ii) Carla, Rebecca and Pamela from the village? The "Three
Marias"? (a very usual group in Spanish).

Konduce las kurvas peligrosas, He drives the dangerous curves,
eskutxando anarko-punk. Pilla correo en Aoiz, llega temprano al
almacén.
listening to anarco-punk. He gets the post in Aoiz, arriving early
at the warehouse.
Le konocen l@s mercaderes y su trato brusko y familiar.
The merchants know him and his brusque and familiar manner.
Sin gastar palabras pide y lleva kajas pesadas de fruta y
verduras,
Without wasting words he asks for carries out heavy boxes of
fruit and vegetables,
kalkula komo kaban en el furgo. El melokotón magullado abrirá
calculating their fit in the van. The bruised peach will open
a descubrir dentro su dulzura.
to reveal inside its sweetness.

2b(ii) Miguel, in the village (whom I admired while he walked up
the path in front of me the previous day) has the same affected
manly nonchalance as Gm. and as he's already involved
heterosexually in the village (a public image which I, Gm., Prince
Edward and Nm. share, superimposed on a previous, simultaneous or
hidden homosexuality) [Miguel was heterosexual : this is wishful
thinking!] the dream wish may be not to be so indiscreet as to
become   emotionally swayed by him. The contrary wish – to get
together discreetly – is also a possible reading.

6c(ii) Absence of seat belts, non-existence of driving licenses and
unpaved roads make car trips an experience of not being in control
of one's own safety.

16a(v) I picked up letters the previous day from the Erkametza
community so I really should have gone [left Chinebro] the day of
the dream.

20(xviii) '*furgonetta*' is 'van' like a transit van.

23 …people had come back from "recycling" food (fruit and veg.
that merchants would throw out)…

24(xiii) I joked a lot here at first about Carla and Rebecca as *jefas*
when I worked with them in the kitchen, until Miguel, jokingly but
also seriously said, "*Aquí no hay jefes*" (Here there are no bosses).
The boss here seems to function as a measure of self-permission and
confidence in my ability. 24(xv) The post is so slow here maybe I

think it's extinct.[77] In Sicily we joked that the mail arrived to Rome by plane and then proceeded by mule.

31(vii) …Maybe there's a connection with the *furgonettas* (the minibuses of the community) here...

NOTES

[77] I'm thinking of Dream 24 (xv) animals as dinosaurs.

Las notxes de san Fermín, The nights of San Fermin,
rellena las kopas kon alegría; kon sonrisa trabaja kon karkajadas de risa
he fills cups with joy; working with a smile and cackles of laughter
y kon ojos mansos kontempla la procesión de hombres y mujeres
and with meek eyes contemplates the procession of men and women
– Anarkist@as Errantes – y les eskutxa, su risa y su llanto,
– errant anarchists – and listens to them, their laughing and their crying,
devolviéndoles el regalo de Santxo Panza a don Kixote:
returning to them the gift of Sancho Panza to don Quixote:
la humilde humanidad. humble humanity.

28(i)…(Ricardo's girlfriend came last night with Enrique who's been away for about two weeks)…

32 (iii) …Pamplona where the group [anarchists visiting Erkametza] comes from – where they have the famous bullrun through the town each year. The festival is called "San Fermin" and the previous night I talked with a girl who'd been in the Gaztetxe (Anarchist Social Centre) in Pamplona the night I had to hitch and walk here in the thunderstorm. That night was "*San Fermin Chiquito*) (Little San Fermin). Posters often show foreigners being gored.

Yo voy haciendo I go on
poemas y panecillos, eskribiendo sueños kolectivos
making sonnets and scones, writing collective dreams
de Erkametzas y Chinebros; bendiciéndo l@s okupas,
maldiciéndo la presa,
of Erkametzas and Chinebros; blessing the okupas and cursing
the dam,
pidiéndo su identidad de los Forales ke nos molestan,
checking the ID of the *Forales* that annoy us,
juntándome kon vosotr@s – perfekt@s anarkist@s –
together with you – perfect anarchists –
¡ke el pueblo se alze para alabaros!
May the people rise up to praise you!

2c(ii) …I arrived at Erkametza wearing my kilt …2c(ix) This
disturbing, zombie-like image of a dead body looking out of a
window haunted me till the following day after starting the
interpretation – I realise now it reminds me of a picture in an EFL
book I used in class in Granada, Spain, about a Caribbean islander
who uses Voodoo to rid his island from unwelcome touristic
development on an old graveyard. The omission of the third person
singular 's' in "he look out of the window" is typical of what in the
USA is known as "Black English", coming from these islands.

6a(ii) The Stations of the Cross are a painful progress uphill (like
two nights previous when I arrived soaked though and scratched by
thorns) but with a goal and a meaning. 6a(iii) This whole dream has
a sense of welcome and arrival.

7a(vii) Here I wear the kilt when I go to Iruñea to busk, it's good
for getting lifts too.

11(xxiii) …I don't want to be seen as an academic here but as an
Anarchist whereas in the Department the reverse is true. What really
interests me is the union of both – as in the "Cracking the
Movement" book (see dream 10a).

12(iii) So it's the left door and the "left-hand path" magic. Later
in the day I was to write to [ ] my supervisor, saying that I'd
considered using magic against the Guardia Civil should they come
to evict us.

14 (i)…– the previous day I started the interpretation of the
recorded dreams, so far I'd only done one and felt that I had a long

way to go until the end (being up to date) as I always felt when walking the Pilgrim's Way to Santiago.

17(xiii) This kind of conversation ["good shit"] is quite normal in the *okupa* villages. Everyone here is white (there are between thirty and fifty of us in six villages) from all parts of Spanish territory and a few from northern Europe. The "three black guys" as well as being racist stereotypes are possibly also shadow figures as drug-taking is something I don't do.

20(xviii) '_____ or bust!' hitchhiking sign. I have several from hitching to Aoiz/ Iruñea...

21a(ii) The previous day I tried to weave some bullrushes into a St. Bridget's cross (a pagan/ Christian symbol) to remember the technique and so weave baskets. It wasn't very successful! 21a(iii) ...I felt very welcomed back and pleased to be here [Erkametza]. 21b(vii) Little irritations? Fleas? Rug rats? Someone said the previous day that I needn't have put all my clothes weighed down with stones under water as fleas only live on animals and carpets.

25(ix) The previous day I wrote a poem about all the members of the community.

26(ii) The previous evening a group of six of us went up to the summit of the mountain (an hour's walk) to go to a cave. We didn't find it in the dark and slept around a campfire, I with a blue plastic bag on my head. I hardly slept with the cold and the stones. This dream is from the day when I came back to Erkametza in the morning and slept till the afternoon. The only thing of red plastic here is the slop bucket which I cleaned in the first few days of being here. My energy was extremely low coming back, I washed, had breakfast and slept immediately to change my mood which could have turned sour. The transformation of the bucket may symbolise this. Red in my dreams has so far symbolised "manly" – in juxtaposition to yellow – but I feel this to be false (plastic).**[78]** Macdonalds use red plastic to make people feel in a hurry – for quicker turnover – as opposed to brown which slows people down.

28(iii) Lf./m. is a transvestite from Brazil and uses the Book of Sao Cipriano (commonly known as "black magic") She has been known to burn houses down by cursing them. Once I felt very involved with her negative energy and had to take ritual action to nullify it. The letter which I received the previous day from the Head of Department at Stirling – going back on his word to pay my keep here and congratulating himself for (finally) paying my £126 plane fare when the other two students on the course were bankrolled to the tune of £2,000 – left me furious and might well have induced me to curse him. 28(vi) At a Hallowe'en party in Brazil I dressed up as a nun – with a black shirt, skirt and a pair of shorts on my head – and looked much better than Valerie who'd spent all day sewing her witch costume. When the party was stopped by order of the local judge – an English student of mine – I remonstrated with the police (who were very respectful as they appeared to be talking to a nun) and said to phone him up and tell him off! I obviously am recalling the switch I did when I took on an authoritarian role with the *Forales* (the "Mounties") and spoke to them as if I were their English teacher.

30(iii)[79] Maybe I'm still thinking about two days ago when I went to Aoiz and had a coffee in a bar and read the newspaper and felt normal. Another time I had the overwhelming urge to buy something – anything – in a garage when hitching back to the community – fed up with gifts and barter and a moneyless economy! 30 (iv) A short story I wrote (after the very successful "Sun on Pale Skin" presentation to the Dept. and before the bitter parody – both based on Harry Potter) involved the "transmogrification" of Harry Potter from White to Black and George Weasley (who's White) putting his arm around Harry after dealing with the evil Draco Malfoy. This image is a reversal, the black guy embraces me (presuming that in the dream I'm White!). 32(i) The previous evening seven members of the local anarchist society came to the village – in a thunderstorm. I made up blanket mattresses for them and Carla cooked. So there was some preoccupation with food and shelter – especially as the roof leaks! 32(viii)… This sexual theme could also link with foreigners being gored and the fact that I was once chased across a field by a herd of bullocks (which they were in the dream) during a discussion on the artificial construction of male/ female roles. In the community we'd made jokes about where they'd sleep and I obviously desired a captive, energetic herd of young virile energy! There is also much insistence on me looking after them (so being more "in" than them, which is what I felt when they arrived.

NOTES

[78] Refers to unincluded ANALYSIS of Dream 3.

[79] Dream 30 I had forgotten (I wonder why?) to analyse in the field and did so only on the 25th July'02 in Stirling.

2: Chinebro

Etnopoesía de Tres Pueblos: Ethnopoetry of Three Villages

Escucho voces I hear voices *vivimos en una iglesia* we live in a
church
y escucho voces and I hear voices
de los muertos enterrados abajo. of the dead buried below.
Reclaman que las campanas no suena más. They complain that
the bells no longer sound. *Hay un hombre en otro pueblo* there is a
man in another village
que sube cada jueves de Huesca who goes up every Thursday
from Huesca
para sonar las campanas to sound the bells
sobre el pantano over the reservoir *que cubre su pueblo* that
covers his village.

11(ii) Chinebro's only roofed building – and only dwelling – is a
stone church in the style of "*Romanico*" (Norman). I have sung here
and played the guitar and tin whistle but also another church
between Erkametza and (just before) Ilargialdi, I visited for its
acoustics.

27(ii) The previous day Ricardo found the poem I'd written in
January while visiting Chinebro. It starts, "I hear voices, I live in a
church and I hear voices…" Most of the *okupa* villages have a
church as their central building – as it's usually in a better state of
repair.

Aquí no hay pantano Here there is no reservoir
Donde hay otros pueblos quieren poner They want to put one on other villages
Pero todavía no ha llegado But it still hasn't come to that
Ojalá que no venga Would to God that it doesn't come
Ojalá que los faraones de Madrid Would to God that the Pharaohs of Madrid
dejen los pueblos del Pirineo en paz leave the people of the Pyranees in peace
y que la buena gente de Valencia and that the good people of Valencia
busquen otro solución look for another solution
así debe ser. that's how it should be. *Ojalá.* Would to God.

2c(ix)…In the 1950's, the Spanish dictator, Franco…[see information on reservoir under *Euzkal Herria*, above]… wanted to encourage even more tourism. An example being the plethora of golf courses in Cádiz – one of the driest provinces of Spain. No doubt the official reason was to stimulate the economy similar to the "New Deal" orchestrated by Roosevelt in the USA. The immediate result was that a handful of contractors became immensely rich – and no doubt were financially grateful to the dictator himself – and thousands of people …[see *Euzkal Herria* above]…The protest of the local people was massive and managed to halt some of the work, sometimes for decades. I don't have information as to when unofficial occupation of the villages began but one village, in a nearby valley, which I have named as "Finko" (the Basque word for "stable/ established" which came into Castilian Spanish as "*finca*" meaning "smallholding") is twenty years old….Of the six *okupa* villages in or near our valley, some are threatened by the water level of the dam itself and some by deforestation. The agencies threatening eviction are the Guardia Civil, the *Forales*, the misnamed company for Repopulation and Housing **[80]** and the Dam company itself. This is a constant theme in the day to day life of the community…

NOTES

[80] My bad translation of "*viviendas*". Literally "living places" it means tree nurseries, not housing.

Llegaron para poner puertas en la iglesia they came to put doors on the church, *gracias*, thanks, *¿han puesto puertas para desalojarnos o abrigarnos?*
Have they put doors to throw us out or to shelter us? *No se.* I don't know.
Esta noche de luna y nieve this night of moon and snow *cuando abro las puertas*
when I open the door *veo Naffaroa en todo su belleza*
I see Navarre in all its beauty, *busco el gato* I look for the cat *y veo que las gallinas están cerradas* and see that the hens are shut in.

25(v) …There are many vultures here and Pancho in Chinebro blames them for the disappearance of the chickens. I think it's because he never shuts the hen house and a fox could have got them or a dog from the nearby village.

No somos muchos There's not many of us *la gente va y viene*
people come and go
y unos se quedan. and some stay. *Trabajamos siempre*: We're
always working:
agricultura, construcción, la casa, los productos, building, the
house, the produce *para el mercado en Iruñea* for the market in
Iruñea.
Vivimos de san Fermín, we live on san Fermin, *de bares, de
obras, de miel, de panadería*, on bars, on construction, on honey, on
baking, *de semillas, de música, de muñecas*, on seeds, on music, on
puppets,
vivimos de gracia y alegría. we live on laughter and joy.

11(viii) These VIPs could also be chess pieces as I was pleased
when Pieter and Pancho played chess as they didn't need language
for that (after Pieter beat me twice).

12(iv) In Erkametza we work very hard physically but here in
Chinebro Pancho has a much more relaxed pace.

21a(i) The previous day I re-met Wendy from S. America, whom
I had met in an *okupa* village last year. She's very pretty and was
living here and there – I invited her to visit us in Erkametza.

Tres pueblos conozco: I know three villages: *Chinebro, Ilargialdi, Pinu,*

Chinebro, Ilargialdi, Pinu. *No suenan campanas en ninguno* no bells sound in any

En Pinu tocan una caracola, In Pinu they sound a conch, *En Ilargialdi llaman*

in Ilargialdi they call, *aquí, pues, decimos,* here, well, we tell each other

porque no somos muchos because we're not many

así sabemos de la cena, that's how we know it's dinnertime.

8(ii) The previous day I walked for two hours to Ilargialdi and from there for another two hours to Chinebro.

14(v) Parable of wheat and darnel? "Thorny bushes" appear on the map Dave from Erkametza drew me to take a shortcut to Chinebro.

16a(i) The previous day we went to Ilargialdi and I was really hungry and wanted to know if they would feed us. We ended up helping ourselves.

20(iii) Four days previously I was really impressed to meet three kids (about 15 years old) who were born in Finko – a squat village 20 years established, the name means "stable". I was openly admiring them thinking what must it be like to be born and grow up in that lifestyle – so natural. See dream 17(iv).

20(viii) Reference to maps that Ricardo and Dave drew me (see thorny bushes, dream 14, comment) to get to Erkametza and Chinebro. Could be references to the other villages especially Azkarra and Ilargialdi.

29(iii) … the kids from Finko (who I didn't actually speak to but seemed really nice).

No rezamos, we don't pray, *cada uno en lo suyo*, each does their own thing
El lee Carlos Castaneda, He reads Carlos Castaneda, *ella es Buddhista*,
she's Buddhist *yo hago masajes energéticos* I do energetic massage. *Puede haber Catolicos*, There could be Catholics *puede haber brujos* there could be witches, *no quemamos a nadie* we don't burn anyone, *hacemos hogueras* we make bonfires
y sentimos nuestro calor humano. and we feel our human warmth.
En Pinu lo tienen sistemado, In Pinu they've got it sorted, *me impresionaron las ventanas de botellas*, the windows of bottles impressed me,
las paredes del baño con cal y cristal quebrado, the walls of the bathroom with limestone and broken glass, *bonitos colores, armonía.* lovely colours, harmony.
En Ilargialdi, menos, In Ilargialdi less,
aquí está todo para hacer. here everything remains to be done.

3(ix) The night before the Twin Towers attack, one American guest had a panic attack. I calmed him with a back/ shoulder/ head massage and an imaginative journey. He said knots in his back and neck he'd had since his father died ten years ago came out and he never stopped thanking me. With Giuseppe, an Italian from the *okupa* village of Pinu, who's no longer here, I had a similar experience.

8(v) Both Ilargialdi and Chinebro have a problem with fleas and tics.

12(vii) "A flea in the ear" probably quite true here in Chinebro…
12(ix) Another expression of desire to go home – either Scotland or Erkametza. 15(iv) I used to be very late for everything and now get impatient with lateness and especially slowness of transitions. Pancho takes ages getting up, having breakfast and smoking and Pieter and I can't do anything because we don't know what to do. 6.30am I got up to pee and thought that that's when the day ought to begin in the country.

16a(iv) Pancho has ["a cold"] and I think he's passed it on to me.

20(ii) This was a sore point in Chinebro as I was constantly cleaning up after people and encouraging people to wash!

20(iv) Pancho washed his hair the other day and looked so much better but the previous day it was all sticking up again. "The Whacky Races" is probably a reference to Pancho's driving. 20(vii) …In fact I respect Finko highly – all I've heard is good. The disdain may be transferred from Chinebro.

21a(ii) …coming back from Chinebro I was quite disgruntled as full of cold with my voice gone.

32 (iv) I did this ["shout at them to go back while I put {the food}in"] with Che, the dog from Chinebro.

Soy teólogo I'm a theologian *veo dedicación* I see dedication
la gente da todo people give everything *cuando entra en la comunidad*
when they enter into the community *comparte comida*, they share
food, *ayuda en obras*, they help each other's work *enseña*
aprendices. they train apprentices *No tiene prejuicios*, they have no
prejudices, *no tiene rivalidad*, no rivalry,
no es capitalista. they're not capitalists.

14(i)…I'd noticed that the hosepipe goes under the road a little…

8(ix) The previous day in Ilargialdi, Sebastian was putting up
boards over their new kitchen ceiling and said he'd put up a Taliban
poster. As I have American friends, I feel a great division of
loyalties.

10a(i) An attempt to distance myself from the events of the Twin
Towers? Pieter from Belgium turned up the previous day and we
discussed the event – for him and most of the *okupa* community it
was a good thing.

10a(xvii) This conclusion doesn't follow from the evidence **[81]**
and makes me think of the car found days after the Twin Towers
attack containing a book on how to fly a plane, the Koran and a
poster of Bin Laden, supposedly of the terrorists. This whole part of
the dream seems to be a collection of disparate elements but I feel
the unifying theme is of Death/ Anarchy/ Occult/ Camp breaking
down rationality and the status quo. The second part develops those
themes. They are also explained in theory and anecdote in the
Cracking the Movement: Squatting Beyond the Media by Adilkno,
the Foundation for the Advancement of Illegal Knowledge, pub.
New York: Autonomedia, 1990. I'd been reading it and the arrival of
Pieter from Belgium (Flanders) made it a topic of conversation.

11(xvi) Obviously wish fulfilment for the comfort and cleanliness
of a hotel.

11(xvii) Our shower is outside and consists of a hose connected to
a metal pipe with a shower head on it. We shower in the afternoon
when the sun has been on the hosepipe (which extends for four
kilometres) and so the water (and our naked bodies) are warmer.
Pieter had a shower the previous day and I stayed inside the house
for his privacy as I don't know him that well.

21b(ix) … reminiscent of …Pieter from Belgium spinning his 'diablos' (devils) in the air and up and down a length of cable strung between two trees.

NOTES

[81] I wouldn't normally associate my (ex)girlfriend with "a pink jumper in process of being knitted and a knapsack and a book in Spanish" [Dream 10a] so "she's here!" doesn't follow.

Sin voto de castidad Without vow of chastity *son cariñosos*, they are loving,
sin voto de pobreza without vow of poverty *comparten todo*, they share everything *sin voto de obediencia* without vow of obedience
están de acuerdo they agree *con lo que decide la asamblea*, with what the assembly decides, *tienen fé*, they have faith, *tienen esperanza*, they have hope, *tienen amor*, they have love *y este suena mejor que una campana.* and that sounds better than a bell.

9(vii) The pantomime could be the ego's social veneer which covers libidinous undercurrents – a desire for Pancho while being charming to his girlfriend.

9(viii) I came to Chinebro to represent Erkametza in the Billera (meeting) which the *okupa* villages hold every few weeks. For me at first it was an excuse to visit Pancho – I'd been in Chinebro for ten days in January when Ricardo, his brother, also lived there …We spent most of the day of the meeting near the Spanish beginning of the Pilgrim's Way to Santiago – picking mushrooms. After a session in the pub no-one was in a condition to drive so everyone stayed here. I slept with Pancho – his girlfriend with two other girls and everybody else wherever they could. I enjoyed snuggling up to him but was conscious in the early morning of the light and greater visibility. I felt he may not want to be seen so close to me. 9(x). I always feel that leaving and arriving in Latin cultures takes so much time: i.e. I'm anxious to be gone from Chinebro.

10a(xv) My girlfriend from Barcelona who I'm having difficulty contacting and hope turns up here.

11(x) The guitar belongs to Angela, Pancho's girlfriend.

13a(i) I did wonder this [where "the guys from Ilargialdi" "could all sleep"] as I invited them to stay after they came back from an anarco-punk festival without Pancho but with Pieter. 13c(i) Om. and Pm., German friends from St. Andrews College, once gave me a basketball lesson which was so successful (given my total emotional block on team sports) that I used it in an essay as an example of good pedagogy. Freud would see this as a reassuring dream that I managed to do something that before I thought impossible.**[82]** I often in the same way dream of my small but intimidating Spanish teacher (I was awful at languages at school) and mentioned this the

previous day to Pieter. I see this as encouragement for the project.
13d(i) Km. is a French friend with whom I shared a flat in Stirling University. As I know a lot of gay people but never "came out" to him and as the Students Association (SUSA) has the reputation of being "a homosexual cabal" we used to joke that I'd enrol him in "The SUSA Club" and so he'd have enough powerful influence to help him with his conflicts with the English Dept. His philological erudition seemed to baffle his tutor and we often had world–weary conversations about the need not to frighten your tutors with how much you know and instead let them patronise you. He is currently translating urban contemporary Scots (Irvine Welsh) into his native tongue Langue d'Oc. He's someone whom I admire greatly, we have experienced similar problems and I hope that my work has similar academic value.

14(xiv) A tall dignified but ironic man from the local village brought Pancho back the previous day, he had a scar on his face and used the plural form (thus including me) when talking about the work that had been done in the village. I realised that to "outsiders" I was now an "insider".

15(ii) The daughter is looking after the mother: as a guest who's doing most of the cooking and cleaning, I'm looking after the resident (and another guest), social relations are inverted.

16a(i) I'd started the analysis of the dreams only a couple of days before this dream (before that I'd only analysed one) and so – intensively reviewing them – I was struck by how much material is sexual and how much of that homoerotic…

16b(vi)…The first part of the dream is slightly embarrassed and sexually implicit. The second part is of performance. When Pablo turned up the previous day – a friend of Pancho's – I was conscious not only of an attraction to him but also a desire to impress him as he is very interesting and artistic.

17(ii) I'm waiting for a letter from my girlfriend and also my family and always check the mailbox when we pass (it's in the village nearby) or the main post office in town. I did both the previous day but only got a letter from the Green Party.

NOTES

[82] See Freud (1888/378) on Typical Dreams: "It would seem, then, that anxious examination dreams… search for some occasion in the past in which great anxiety has turned out to be unjustified and has been contradicted by events."

Bibliography

Adilkno, the Foundation for the Advancement of Illegal Knowledge (1990) *Cracking the Movement: Squatting Beyond the Media*. Autonomedia: New York.

Agar, Michael H. (1996) *The Professional Stranger: An Informal Introduction to Ethnography*. London: Academic Press.

Barley, Nigel (1986) *The Innocent Anthropologist: Notes from a Mud Hut*. Harmondsworth, Middlesex, Penguin. 1st Pub. in Penguin (1986). 1st Pub. (1983) London: British Museum Publications.

Barry, Peter (1995) *Beginning Theory: An Introduction to Literary and Cultural Theory*. Manchester: Manchester University Press.

Bell, Shannon (1993) "Kate Bornstein: A Transgender Transsexual Postmodern Tiresias" in Arthur & Marilouise Kroker (Eds) *The Last Sex: Feminism and Outlaw Bodies* London: MacMillan, Culture Texts, pp 104–120.

Buzan, Tony (1988) Make the Most of Your Mind. (1st ed. 1977) London: Sydney & Auckland, Pan Books.

Cesara, Manda (1982) *Reflections of a Woman Anthropologist: No Hiding Place*. London: Academic Press.

Clifford Geertz (2000) *Available Light: Anthropological Reflections on Philosophical Questions*. Princeton, New Jersey: Princeton University Press.

Clifford, James (1997) *Routes: Travel and Translation in the Late Twentieth Century*. London: Harvard University Press.

Cohen, Anthony P. (1994) *Self Consciousness: An Alternative Anthropology of Identity*. London & New York: Routledge.

Crews, Fredrick (and his critics). (1995) *The Memory Wars: Freud's Legacy in Dispute.* New York: New York Review of Books.

Culler, Jonathan (1997) Literary Theory: *A Very Short Introduction.* Oxford: Oxford University Press.

Donner, Florinda (1982) *Shabono.* New York: Dell.

Edgar, Iain Ross (1994) *Imaginary Fields: The Cultural Construction of Dream Interpretation in Three Contemporary British Dream Groups.* Ph.D. in Social Anthropology, University of Keele. Published on Internet. 7/27/02
http://sapir.ukc.ac.uk/Guests/g–ie/cultdream.thesis.html

Fetterman, David M. (1998) *Ethnography Step by Step.* Thousand Oaks, California: Sage.

Fichte, Hubert (1987) *Etnopoesía: Antropologia Poética das Religiões Afro-Americanas.* São Paulo: Brasiliense.

Freud, Sigmund (1977) *The Interpretation of Dreams* (The Pelican Freud Library, No.4, General Eds. Angela Richards, Albert Dickson) reprinted (1976). Middlesex: Penguin.

Freud, Sigmund (1988) *Art & Literature* (The Pelican Freud Library, No.14 General Eds. Angela Richards, Albert Dickson) reprinted (1985, 1986). Middlesex: Penguin.

García Moriyon, Félix (1992, 2nd ed.) *Del Socialismo Utópico al Anarquismo.* Madrid: Editorial Cincel Kapelusz. (1st ed.1985) Madrid: Editorial Cincel S.A.

Greenblatt, Stephen (1984) *Renaissance Self-Fashioning: From More to Shakespeare.* Paperback ed. 1st edition (1984) Chicago & London: University of Chicago Press.

Harmon, Louise (2013) "Going Back to a Place Where You Once Led a Life: Rereading *Zen and the Art of Motorcycle Maintenance*" in James R. Elkins (Ed.) *The Legal Studies Forum* Vol. XXXVII, Suppl.1. pp.7-36.

Hetherington, Kevin (2000) *New Age Travellers: Vanloads of Uproarious Humanity* London & New York: Cassell.

Hooper, John (1995) *The New Spaniards*. London: Penguin.

Internet Anarchist University
http://www.infoshop.org/iau/today.html

Kitcher, Patricia (1992) *Freud's Dream: A Complete Interdisciplinary Science of Mind.* Cambridge, MASS & London: MIT Press.

Lewin, Kurt (1967) *Field Theory and Social Science: Selected Theoretical Papers*. Ed. Dorothy Cartwright. Social Science Paperbacks: London.

Llobera, Josep R. (1990, 2nd, amplified ed.) *La Identidad de la Antropología*. Barcelona: Anagrama (Poscriptum). *La Reconstrucción de la Antropología* Spanish version lightly corrected and brought up to date of the original English, presented at the VI Congress of Anthropology in the Spanish State (Tenerife, 1993). (1st ed. 1999).

Malatesta, Enrico & Morton Jr., James F. (1900) *Anarchy: Is it all a Dream*? Free Society Library, No.5, June. San Fransisco: A.Isaak.

Marcus, George E. (1998) *Ethnography through Thick and Thin*. New Jersey: Princeton University Press.

McCarthy Brown, Karen (1991) *Mama Lola*. Berkeley, Los Angeles & London: University of California Press.

McManus, Alan (2015) "Strange Attractors: Myth, Dream, and Memory in Educational Methodology" in Paul Smeyers, David Bridges, Nicholas C. Burbules & Morwena Griffiths (Eds) *International Handbook of Interpretation in Educational Research* (Vol. 2). Dordrecht, Heidelberg, NY, London: Springer. pp.1571-1593.

McManus, Alan (2011) *Alchemy at the Crossroads: Pirsig, Pedagogy and the Metaphysics of Quality*, available at www.robertpirsig.org.
Meddis, Ray (1977) *The Sleep Instinct*. London, Henley & Boston: Routledge & Kegan Paul.

Osborne, Richard (1993) *Freud for Beginners*. New York & London: Writers and Readers Publishing Inc.

Paglia, Camille (1990) *Sexual Personae: Art and Decadence from Nefertiti to Emily Dickenson*. London: Penguin.

Pirsig, Robert M. (1974) *Zen and the Art of Motorcycle Maintenance: An Inquiry into Values*. London, Vintage.

Rowling, Joanna K. (2000) *Harry Potter and the Goblet of Fire*. London: Bloomsbury.

Rynkiewich, Michael A. (1976) "The Underdevelopment of Anthropological Ethics" in Michael A. Rynkiewich & James P. Spradley (Eds.) *Ethics and Anthropology: Dilemmas in Fieldwork* (pp. 47–60) Wiley. New York & London.

Teish, Louisa (1986) *Jambalaya*. London: HarperCollins.

Webster, Richard (1995) *Why Freud was Wrong: Sin, Science and Psychoanalysis*. London: HarperCollins.

Wolf, Margery (1992) *A thrice-told tale: feminism, postmodernism, and ethnographic responsibility*. Stanford, Calif.: Stanford University Press.

Young, Robert (1995) *Colonial Desire: Hybridity in Theory, Culture, and Race*. London & New York: Routledge.

About the Author

Alan McManus, M.Theol.(hons), M.Phil, PGDE, M.Litt., Ph.D., is a freelance academic, novelist, playwright and dramaturg. His doctoral thesis, *Alchemy at the Chalkface: Pirsig, Pedagogy and the Metaphysics of Quality,* is on the work of the creative and contrarian American Philosopher, Dr Robert M. Pirsig. *Only Say The Word: Affirming Gay and Lesbian Love*, published by Christian Alternative in 2013, is the first in a planned series of considerations of the ethical implications of his reading of pirsigian metaphysics (ontology) and is followed by *Life Choice: the Ethics and Ideologies of Abortion*. He has also published articles on political philosophy and WW1 remembrance in the online journal, *Citizenship, Social and Economics Education*. He has published two novellas and one novel of his Bruno Benedetti Mysteries, a series of inclusive stories set in Glasgow, with another forthcoming. His twitter address is @gumptionology.

About the Author's work

"In a bravura narrative of his own highly personalised odyssey through graduate studies, McManus places receptivity to learning at the centre of qualitative research. but it is a receptivity open to traditions of though, study and self-examination often marginal to Western rationalism in even its most postmodern and ludic forms. Accessing dreams, esoteric knowledge, literature, myth, and a metaphysics, McManus seeks to raise transgression to the level of an art tempered only by the moral seriousness of the researcher-adventurer invested in the fortunes of the marginalized and the forgotten."

(Prof. Robert A. Davis, Head of School of Education, University of Glasgow, in the Introduction to McManus 2015)

"The author accompanies the reader in a sophisticated network of reflections on homosexuality, on violence, or child abuse, through an extremely eclectic and original approach of cultural references ranging from ethics to spirituality, from philosophy to metaphysics, from philology to biblical exegesis. Creative writing is not lacking: into the nonfiction prose the author interweaves a "rainbow of churches", one for each colour of Pride, seven different denominations presented on the basis of how the gay community is welcomed inside. A book that requires careful reading and some little effort from the reader, but which at the same time offers a new way, firstly logical and rational, then spiritual, of tackling issues that, commonly regarded as taboo, are often set aside."

(Luca, review on www.goodreads.com)

"Sweeping aside centuries of hypocrisy, Alan McManus shines a light on the motives of biblical scholars in their approach to the most important religious question of the day. So many words have been written about homosexuality – these words are actually worth reading."

(The Very Rev Kelvin Holdsworth, Provost of the Episcopal Cathedral Church of St Mary the Virgin, Glasgow, Scotland. Endorsement on www.christian-alternative.com/books/only-say-word)